# Homeless is not Hopeless

John Fritz

Published by
Lion in the Park Press
St. Paul, Minnesota
55105

*Dedicated to my two sons, Jeremy and Joshua,*
*and to all those who have shown me kindness*
*throughout my life.*

# Contents


| | |
|---|---|
| Preface | vii |
| Childhood | 1 |
| Drunk at 12 | 23 |
| Homeless at Sixteen | 40 |
| Married, with Children | 66 |
| The Good Times | 88 |
| Hard Times on the Road | 125 |
| Prison | 150 |
| Trying to Quit | 169 |
| Recovery | 184 |

My desire to tell my story of alcoholism, homelessness and a crisis of failures became a goal after completing five years of sobriety and a successful reunion with my children. It's an honest story which could have ended differently but for the kindness of strangers and a certain amount of inherited physical fortitude. I begin with my early life in northern Minnesota.

These are my words describing my actual experiences. It is my true story. Over a period of months, I told this story into a tape recorder with my friend David Koehler who key stroked a transcript and helped me organize the material into this book.

# 1

# Childhood

## Hitting bottom

I was flying a sign on Snelling Avenue in St. Paul with my buddy Boo. The next thing I knew I woke up in a ditch in St. Paul along I-94 and University Avenue. I was empty, so empty.

I wanted to die, and I was too scared to kill myself. So, I walked down to the Union Gospel Mission. This is something I never, ever did. I never went to missions. But that night I walked down to the mission and starting talking to the chaplain. He convinced me to go to the mental health unit. It was April 20, 2010. I wound up at Regions Hospital.

After I was in the hospital for a few days I wanted to check myself out. I had checked myself in, and I thought they would let me go. "No," they said, "You are too much of a mess. We are going to put a 72-hour hold on you or we will commit you."

They got me back on medication. I was there 17 days. They said I could go into treatment if I wanted to. I really didn't think that would do any good. I thought there was no sense in going. I thought treatment was a complete waste of time. After all I had been in and out of treatments centers 16 times already. What would be different this time? But I thought, "Well, at least I'll get out of this mental health unit. Once I'm at the treatment center, I can just walk away."

I got to the treatment center, and I wasn't sure what to do. I had arrived late in the day. I decided, "Well, I'll stay the night."

But then I did something I can't explain, something I had not done in years. I got down on my knees. I said a prayer to something. I don't know what it is. I said, "God, I don't know what you are, but I can't do this anymore."

I got up and picked up this book that was sitting there. It was the Alcoholics Anonymous "big book." I opened it at random. I had opened it to page 437. It had a story called, "My bottle, My Resentment and Me." I started to read. It was the true story of a hobo who had been drinking all his life, and he sobered up. What were the odds of me opening this book to this story? It was my story. The guy was telling my story. I realized that if he could do it, maybe I could do it.

I decided to give sobriety one more attempt. The only reason I was in that treatment center was to escape the mental health unit. But now after I read that story, there was something different. My obsession to drink seemed to be lifted from me at that point. For years I had been obsessed with drinking. Every waking hour I was either drinking or thinking about drinking. But now it seemed different. I was not obsessed about drinking.

That was an important day. It started me on the path of becoming a new man.

Now it is six years later. I want to share my story. It's a story that I don't fully understand. Although I don't consider myself a religious man, this is a story marked by some miracles as well as many simple acts of kindness by men and women in my life.

I want to tell my story because maybe I can be a spokesman for homeless people. We have a story to tell. Perhaps it will provide some insights for good people who are trying to help the homeless. And maybe this story can help someone. If it helps one homeless person turn their life around, it will be worth it to me.

### Let's start at the very beginning

I wasn't born homeless. I became homeless. So let me start out at the beginning with my early childhood growing up in a blue collar family in rural northern Minnesota. I was born in Bagley, Minnesota on August 1, 1959. I was named Randy John. I was the last of six children born to Bill and Beryl Fritz.

The six of us children were born in a short span of 8 years. The oldest child was my sister, Bev. Then there was Bill the oldest boy, then Bruce, then Bob and Bud who was just two years older than me. One girl and then five boys. I was the only one in the family whose first name did not begin with "B," but that is another story.

My mother grew up on a farm in northern Minnesota. Her parents were Michael and Blanche Poppler. My mother, Beryl, was born in 1931, the eighth of nine children. It was a loving family. Eventually they moved to Lengby. My father was born in 1927 near Barron, Wisconsin. His parents were Alex and Dora Fritz. They were poor farmers. Dad was sent out to do a man's job on a dairy farm when he was only 12. His father was a violent alcoholic. In fact, as far back as we can trace, all the Fritz men were alcoholics.

Somehow my mother and father met, and they were married in 1950. They settled in the tiny town of Lengby. Our family lived in Lengby, Minnesota until I was in first grade. Lengby is located in northern Minnesota 100 miles from the Canadian border and 70 miles from North Dakota. It was farming country, and we lived on a small farm. This is dairy country, and we had some cows that we milked by hand. Apparently the farm was not enough to support the family because both my mother and father worked at a plant where they made potato chips. We called it the "potato house."

There were good times growing up in my family. We never had a lot of money, but there was always enough to eat. My mom was a great cook. My older brothers and my older sister kind of

**My mother, Beryl Poppler (aged 20) with her mother and father, Blanche and Michael Poppler**

protected me because I was the baby of the family. In fact, one time my sister Bev saw this kid bullying me. She just beat him up.

### BURYING MY TEDDY BEAR

I had blonde hair. It was almost white. I suppose I was a cute little boy. I couldn't have been more than three years old when I had a teddy bear that I loved. I carried that teddy bear around, and I slept with that teddy bear. I remember our dog tearing up my teddy bear. I cried. I just bawled. So Bud and I had a funeral for the teddy bear. We dug a grave in the garden where the soil was loose and buried the teddy bear. It was in our berry garden where we had raised blackberries, raspberries and strawberries.

I remember the time my dad took me fishing in Solberg

**My father and mother, Bill and Beryl Fritz, in about 1969**

Creek—an outlet for Lengby Lake. I was about four. My sister and all my brothers were in school. It was just Dad and I. The sunfish were spawning. We had two rods. I was pulling out sunfish as fast as my dad could take them off and re-bait the lines. He was just ecstatic.

We didn't have running water on the farm in Lengby. But nearby was a pipe sticking out of the side of a hill, and water flowed out of it. It was a natural spring. We'd go there and fill up ten-gallon creamery cans and lug them to the house. We had an outhouse down the hill from the house. We used "honey buckets." It was a five-gallon pail that you could use when it was cold. Otherwise you went outside to go to the outhouse.

We also had a stream running through the farm that the cows could drink out of. We didn't have to worry about getting water for them. When it froze in the winter, we chopped holes in the ice.

We took baths once a week in a big washtub. My mother heated some water on the stove and then set the tub on top of a big grate in the floor. The grate was over the woodstove in the basement, and the heat came up through that grate. Bev got to go first because she was a girl. Then I got to bathe next because I was the little one. By the time it got to the sixth kid, that water was pretty nasty.

I remember riding the school bus when I was living in Lengby. We rode the bus to school in Fosston. John Vig and I were in the same grade. I would get on the bus before him, and I couldn't wait for John to get on the bus so I had somebody to talk with—somebody who was my own age. John and I were fast friends for years—even after I moved away from Lengby.

### Three Years Old and Sipping Hamm's Beer

At times my father found me amusing. I was two or three years old when I took the first drink out of my dad's beer can. I remember him drinking Hamm's beer. I think he thought it was funny.

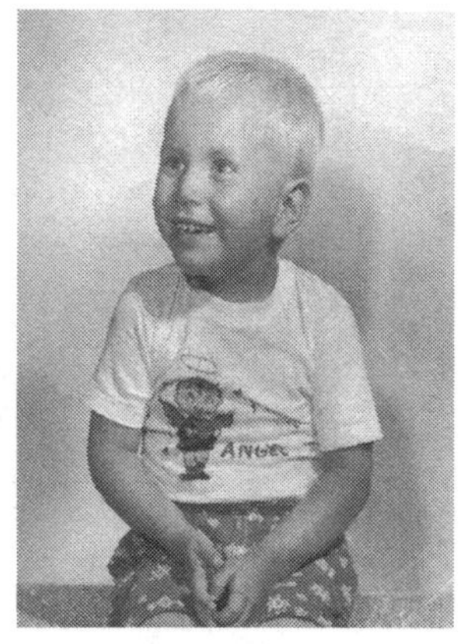

**I am three years old in this professional portrait.**

At Christmas time in 1965 we moved from Lengby to McIntosh. It was in the middle of first grade. The first day of school in McIntosh, there was this kid sitting in front of me, and he kept turning around asking, "What's your name again?" His name was Kevin Johnson, and it turned out that I lived next door to him. We walked home from school together that day. We were immediately best friends.

### Our house

Our new house was on the south side of town—the fifth house from the railroad tracks. I learned that we lived on the wrong side of the tracks. The address was 530 Cleveland Avenue which was also County Highway 41. It was a frame house painted an ugly yellow. There was a big front porch with all glass windows. It was built around the turn of the century. From the porch you entered through the front door right into the dining room where we had a big dining room table. Also on the first floor was the living room, kitchen and Mom and Dad's bedroom. The bathroom was between the bedroom and the kitchen with doors to each. Then there was a stairway to the upstairs where there were two bedrooms and some big walk-in closets.

There were two big cottonwood trees in the front yard, and we created a huge garden in the back—as big as a football field.

**The Fritz family house in McIntosh**

The best part of this house was running water. You turned the faucet handle and the water came out. You could choose hot water or cold water. It was a whole new world to me. The first time I got in the tub to share a bath with Bud, I turned on more hot water and the handle got stuck. I shouted, "The hot got stuck. The hot got stuck." Everyone teased me. But I got terrified of the hot water. I hardly dared turn it on after that.

We heated the house with a wood stove in the living room. My older brothers chopped the wood. By the time I was nine years old, it was my job to carry all the firewood inside. Every week during the winter I filled our back porch with firewood to keep that stove burning.

Our new town had a population of about 800 people in those days. We had four churches and two bars plus a 3.2 bar. This is a bar that is only allowed to sell "near beer"—with no more than 3.2% alcohol. The VFW also had a bar, so drinking was plentiful in our town.

McIntosh was located in the middle of farming country surrounded by small dairy farms.

When I was a kid a family farm of no more than a half section (320 acres) could support a family of ten.

We had a creamery where the farmers took their cans of milk.

There was a co-op gas station, two small grocery stores, Pierson's Five and Dime where you could buy anything from a Matchbox car to buttons and clothes. The meat market was well known throughout the area. We had a weekly newspaper, the McIntosh Times where you could keep up with the local gossip. There was also a hardware store. If you needed something Harold would find it for you or could get it in a couple days. There were two car dealerships—Ford and Mopar. It was fairly prosperous in the 1960's. There was also a mortuary right on main street. When I went across town to play with my friend Larry, I would have to be home around dark. That meant I had to walk down a dark street or walk right by the mortuary. I was scared of the dark because my brothers thought it was funny to scare me. Anyway I would walk by the mortuary singing or whistling to pretend I wasn't scared.

**This school photo shows me in first grade, the year we moved from Lengby to McIntosh, Minnesota.**

## Mom

My mom was a gentle soul. One of my earliest memories goes back to when I was about three years old, sitting in her lap. I would be tired or cranky, and she would softly stroke my eyelashes to get me to close my eyes and go to sleep.

I remember coming home from school to homemade bread right out of the oven, and we would spread melted butter on it. Uuummmm, that was good. Mom baked twice a week. If we were real lucky Mom would make cinnamon rolls.

Mom called me Johnny. She was the only one who ever did that. It made me feel special. I was sick a lot as a kid. I remember

Mom doted over me—making sure I had everything I needed—juice, ice cream, soup, being warm enough. Because I was home a lot, Mom taught me to bake. I was good at it. I learned to make home-made cakes, cookies and other goodies. The only thing I couldn't master was bread. I didn't have the patience for it.

My mom was a very tolerant woman. She let Kevin and Ronnie (Kevin's nephew who was also our same age), and me pretend to be a rock band. Everybody else was gone. We were about nine at the time. We had a Gerard stereo that I was too young to use. She let us play it for the first time that night. We draped the lamp shade with a cloth of some kind for mood lighting. We put a bunch of Bev and Bill's 45 rpm records on the stereo. We got up on the couch and chairs. Voila! We were on stage. We sang to the music. In our imagination we were famous rock stars. Mom let us stay up late that night. I felt like a grown-up.

Later when I finished fourth grade I was real sick. I spent about 10 days in the hospital in Grand Forks. I found out later they were treating me for leukemia. My sister, Bev, graduated high school that year, and she was working in Grand Forks, so she would visit me every night. Mom had to be home with the other brothers and for her work. Most of the time when I was growing up in McIntosh, Mom worked at the local nursing home. Mom bought me a Teddy Bear and gave it to me at the hospitals, which was special because we rarely got presents.

That summer Mom was worried about me—scared that she might lose me. So, she gave me a big birthday party. It was the only birthday party I ever had. I invited about 20 kids over, and she set up big picnic tables in the backyard. We had hot dogs, cake, you name it. Mom went all out. I was so happy.

I remember one Christmas I was searching around under the Christmas tree trying to find the present that was for me. I found it and accidentally poked a finger through the paper and saw that it was Hot Wheels. I put the present back and immediately went into the kitchen and told my mom that what I was hoping to get for Christmas that year was Hot Wheels. I wanted to make her feel good.

### Dad

My dad had a rough childhood. He grew up poor, the second of six kids. He was the oldest son and grew up in a very violent home. He was required to work a man's job on a dairy farm when he was 12 years old. He hated his father, and he hated his mother as well. Eventually his parents got a divorce.

Dad didn't have a regular job when we moved to McIntosh. Then he started driving a truck—hauling grain to the Dakotas and to Duluth. He got a DWI, and he lost his job driving a truck for a while. That was in the 1960's when you had to work hard to get a DWI in rural Minnesota. Dad always drank. He claimed that he wasn't an alcoholic, but he drank a lot. Finally, he got a job at Land O Lakes. He hauled bulk milk for them. He drove from creamery to creamery picking up milk and delivering it. I think he felt that he came from nothing in Wisconsin, and now he was doing something here in Minnesota. He worried about what people said about him and his family. For instance, he insisted that we all go to church. He didn't go to church, but he wanted us to go to church to make him look good.

When I was in about seventh grade, a revival came to town. Dad took us all. He made us all go up and commit ourselves to Jesus. He sat at the back and watched us. We didn't have a choice because he would have beaten us up if we didn't.

Dad was a big man—he was 6 foot three and weighed about 250 pounds. He could be really intimidating. He was aware of it, and he took advantage of that intimidation factor.

Dad was hard working. He had to work hard when he was a child. He wanted his boys to be working all the time. I think he was lonely. He didn't seem to have any friends. And he was angry. There was usually anger simmering under the surface—even when

**My father wanted his family to look respectable. Here we are in a 1968 family portrait. In the back row are Bev (17) and Bill (15). In the second row are Dad and Mom and me (9). In the front row are Bud (11), Bruce (13), and Bob (12). Notice how everyone has short, neatly groomed hair.**

everything seemed to be going well. For instance, he would take us fishing and we would be having a good time, and all of a sudden somebody would say something and wham. He would hit one of us. We were little kids, and he hit us with a hard slap.

He didn't seem to have a normal sense of humor. He didn't laugh at the usual things. He laughed at strange things. I remember he would sometimes come home from work, reach into his pocket, pull out a handful of change and fling it across the floor. My three younger brothers and I would dive for it and fight for the coins. Dad would sit back and laugh. He seemed to like to see us fight. One year he got us all boxing gloves for Christmas so he could watch us beat up each other.

It was very important to him that we all look respectable. In the family portrait that was taken of all of us in 1968, you can see he had a crew cut and everyone else has short, neatly groomed hair. Long hair for boys seemed to represent the "outlaw" element in his mind, and it became symbolic of his control over us.

He had a dream of having his own small farm. I don't know what happened to the farm in Lengby. When we got settled in McIntosh he saved up his money and bought 40 acres outside of town where he got a horse, raised a few pigs and so on. It seemed like this is where he spent his money. My mother was working at the local nursing home, and she spent her earnings supporting the family—buying groceries and making sure we had a present at Christmas time.

### There were good times

From the time I was six until I was about 12, there were a lot of good times. There were some good times at school. I had good friends. My brothers and I had fun together. I even had good times with my father.

My school in McIntosh was the biggest building in town. It was a big red brick building, three stories high with a one-story addition. The high school was in the one-story addition. There was an old gym and a new gym. The old gym had a stage with huge purple curtains. The stage was used for grade-school plays. My class had 15—20 kids in it, so the whole school from kindergarten to seniors was maybe 250 kids.

Each year our classroom teacher would give us the Iowa Basic Test. It tested your intelligence and where you were in school. We were tested every year. I did extremely well. They said I was in the top three percentile in the state as far as my intelligence level. But I never applied myself. I did just enough to get by.

My mom and dad expected more of me. I didn't want to be this kid that was super smart. I just wanted to hang out with my friends. I was especially good in math. It just kind of came natural to me. When I was in seventh grade, I was actually helping the teacher teach algebra. I would take three or four kids. They would sit at my table, and I would show them how to do the formulas. Some of them were cute girls too.

When I was in second grade, we had a Christmas project. We were melting crayons making colorful things. I did a Christmas tree with all different colored lights on it—all with melted crayons. It was about 18" by 24." My teacher was Mrs. Ruud, and she was very proud of it. She just doted on how well I had done. I took it home and gave it to my mother as a Christmas present.

Lunch was served on tables set up in the old gym which was connected to the school kitchen. For lunch there was always a lot of food—plenty of buttered white bread and often peanut butter and honey sandwiches. One of my favorite meals was mashed potatoes and hamburger gravy. I was one of the smaller boys in my class, but I could out-eat everybody except Curtis who was a big, fat kid.

We would walk through the line and have our card punched for meals. With six kids in the family, we qualified for reduced price lunches. It kind of embarrassed me, so in fourth grade Kevin and I decided to earn our lunches. We got the job of setting up tables and pouring milk in exchange for lunches. I wanted to earn my lunch rather than get a hand-out.

There were always sandwiches left over from lunch. The first and second grades took an afternoon snack of sandwiches and milk—some days even chocolate milk. I remember how we looked forward to this—hoping there would be peanut butter and honey left. I recall the dried out bread that was just starting to get a little hard. I liked it.

We kept a horse and a few pigs on the 40 acre farm that Dad got just outside of town. The horse was named Charlie, and Charlie was an ornery horse. I remember trying to ride him one time. He bucked me off, and somebody had to help me climb back on. I was maybe ten years old at the time and was riding bareback. I never told Dad about this because I was scared that I would be in trouble.

One year Dad built us a baseball field on the property behind our house. Dad and the local blacksmith built a backstop and the whole works. We neighborhood kids had a place to play ball on our side of town.

### Fritz and Sons Garbage Collection

The guy who was the garbage collector in town was drunk all the time, so my dad got us the job. He had an older FarmAll Tractor that was built in the 1940's. We got a wagon and hitched it up, and we took over the garbage collection business in town. Once Dad secured the route for us, we did all the work.

We were only in grade school or junior high at the most, but Bruce, Bob and Bud took over the route, driving the tractor. Sometimes my brothers would get in fights with each other. The old man would get so mad about that. "If you want to fight go out to the dump and fight. Don't fight where people can see you."

I was in fourth grade, and I was put in charge of collections. At the end of each month I knocked on doors and collected the monthly garbage collection fee. I kept track of the books. Dad always wanted me to go into business.

The dump was about a half mile outside of town. We drove the tractor out there and dumped the garbage. Sometimes Kevin and I could go out there with our 22's and shoot rats.

Sometimes we would dig through the garbage and find wonderful stuff. You'd never know what you would find in the garbage. My brother Bob one time found a bag full of $900. It was a bank bag and belonged to the people who owned the bakery. They never would have known what happened if we didn't bring them that bag. They gave Bob a $20 reward.

Every summer we looked forward to Crazy Days. They were wonderful. All the stores would set up tables on the sidewalk in front of the store and sell things. There were only about ten stores in town, but for us it was a big deal. All the farm kids came to town so we got to see friends you hadn't seen all summer.

We always had a big garden. It was an acre in size. We grew everything but potatoes. All of us kids worked in that garden. I weeded. You go up and down a row and pick weeds. Mom did a lot of canning in those days. She canned green beans and corn. She even canned venison and chicken.

For crazy days our family had a booth. We sold cabbages and corn on the cob. I was in charge of the booth. I took in the money and made change. Of course, we had to pay Dad for the seed and stuff. We didn't get nothing free. I was 10 years old at the most when I started selling stuff at our booth.

One summer the local dry goods store, Gordy's Goodies, had a sidewalk sale offering a bunch of Aussie army caps in psychedelic colors. I bought a purple one, and when I got home, Bruce said he liked it. I sold it to him for a dime more than I had paid for it. Then I bought another; I wound up selling that to Bob for a dime more. The next thing you know, I got a business going selling hats for Gordy. All the boys in town were wearing these wild colored Aussie hats.

We had potato fights. We would go to the potato house. I was about nine years old. The potato house was a big, flat building for the raw storage of potatoes. They had bagged potatoes there in 100-pound bags. They loaded these on railroad cars. They didn't process potato chips or anything.

The building had five bays that were over 100 feet deep. They piled raw potatoes as high as the ceiling. We would crawl up over them. You find these nice little potatoes. We'd throw them at each other. When you got hit by a potato, it hurt.

Sometimes we'd bring a salt shaker with us, peel a potato and eat it raw.

### Dad taught us to swim

Dad taught us to swim in Lengby Lake. He taught all five of us boys. This was after we moved to McIntosh. He got in the water with us. Dad was really good at this. He taught each one of us to swim. He would hold us with his hand and have us paddle our arms and then let us go. I was about six. My mom would be on the beach watching us—making sure we didn't get too crazy. The swimming test was that you had to swim out around the tower (which was in the lake about 50 feet from shore) and then swim back to shore. It was six or seven feet deep swimming around that tower. Once we passed the swimming test we could swim wherever we wanted to.

One day we were playing with our BB guns, and my brother Bob told me I had to go home. I was sick and tired of being told I had to go home. So, I shot him. Then I ran home to tell Mom before he could tell her.

Danny Bok lived at the south end of town. Right across from him was this old abandoned house. It had no paint—just dilapidated. We were playing with our BB guns and accidentally we shot out a window in the house. Danny had two BB guns. We had a pellet gun. Ronnie had his own BB gun. So we decided to finish the job. We started shooting and we shot all the windows out of the house.

It turned out the house belonged to one of the crankiest old men in town—Evil Howgan. Of course we got in trouble for that. Evil was not only cranky, he was one of the town drunks. I remember hearing two other old drunks—Gus and Palmer. They were bachelor farmers. They coaxed cranky old Evil Howgan saying, "Evil, Evil. Give the boys some candy."

I had a lot of friends. Kevin Johnson was my best friend, but other friends were Danny Defrang, Bobby Finkle, Danny Bak and David Gelldocker. We called him "Jelly Roll."

I liked it when I was good at something—almost anything. I

learned to tie my shoes early. In fact, my brother Bud was two years older than me, and I taught him how to tie his shoes.

One Christmas my present was this stick with a saucer thing. You could make that saucer spin on the stick if you did it just right. I could do it before any of my brothers. That made me proud.

The Fritz boys had a reputation for doing anything to earn money. We milked cows. We baled hay. We mowed lawns. We did almost anything. My brothers had the town paper route to deliver the Crookston Daily Tribune and the Grit. When I was in second grade they figured I was old enough, and they turned the route over to me. I delivered the papers and had to collect the money at the end of each week.

**My best friend, Kevin Johnson**

Dad took us fishing, and he seemed to be a different person. It was like he was two different people. He would take us up to Red Lake to go fishing. We didn't have a boat or anything. We just fished from the shore. But he spent time with us. Sometimes they were good times. He took us camping. He played baseball with us.

One time the whole family went to Lengby Lake. The plan was for all of us to go swimming and then have a picnic lunch. There was a big picnic table, and we had a bunch of fried chicken. We put it on the table and went swimming. When we returned, there was a bunch of little Indian kids. They had eaten all the food. But what I especially remember is that nobody got super upset about it—not even Dad. We figured those Indian kids needed the food more than we did.

### Sylvia's 3.2 bar

We had plenty of places to drink in McIntosh. There was a liquor store, and there were two bars. People stuck to the same bar, and they had their favorite spot in the bar. There are probably people today still sitting on the same chair where they were sitting 50 years ago. There was also the VFW crowd. They had their own bar at the VFW club. Finally, there was Sylvia's. That was a 3.2 bar—where they couldn't sell anything stronger than beer that was 3.2% alcohol. It was open on Sundays when other places were closed. So that was the place to be on Sunday nights.

There was a big mirror behind the bar with cigarettes and candy bars and potato chips and the till. The bar had this beer bar smell. There is no way to explain the smell unless you actually smelled it. You could smell the stale beer and the cigarette smoke and the hamburgers that were cooking—all kind of mingled together. It was kind of a good smell in a way. It really was. It was comforting in a way because it was something you knew.

**Each afternoon Kevin Johnson and I raced all the way to my house after school to watch *Dark Shadows* on TV. It was a scary soap opera with werewolves and vampires.**

There were a couple of pinball machines and a shuffle board game in there. You could have "set ups." She couldn't sell liquor, but you could bring your own bottle. You gave it to Sylvia. She'd write your name on it and put it under the bar. Then she'd sell you a drink out of it. She'd mix it with soda pop or some mix and mix you a drink using your liquor. So, you're actually paying for your booze twice.

I remember Dad taking me to Sylvia's when I was about nine years old. He ordered two beers and gave me one. He got really mad because I started playing pinball. "You don't waste your money on that," he shouted. I guess he wanted me sitting next to him drinking my beer.

Kevin and I used to run home from school to my house to watch *Dark Shadows* on our television set. It was a soap opera featuring vampires. We ran home every day. We would sit on the floor close to the black and white, 19" Zenith TV that Dad bought in 1955. Sometimes we ate peanut butter sandwiches. We wouldn't miss that program. We didn't get color TV until 1975.

### Things weren't always good

Dad insisted that things be done his way. My brothers and I learned that there were three ways of doing something—the right way, the wrong way, and Dad's way. It had to be done Dad's way. One time he woke me up in the middle of the night and said that I didn't stack the firewood in the back porch correctly—his way. I had to get up and go down and rearrange the wood pile to suit him.

Just after we moved to McIntosh when I was six years old, I remember Mom hiding in the closet. I brought her a blanket there to see if I could help her. Obviously it was over violence, but I don't remember much of it.

I came home one time and the whole house was destroyed. Everything was tipped over, kicked around, books scattered, pictures knocked off the wall, tables turned over. That's one of the times that Mom left. For many years Mom and Dad were off and on. Sometimes he moved out. Sometimes she moved out.

Sometimes Dad would come into the house swinging. He hit my mom and started hitting my older brothers. He choked Mom. My brothers started to defend her. So he turned on them. He would come home and raise holy hell. Three of them—Mom and two older brothers—would unite against Dad. Then he figured out that he couldn't beat three of them. So, he would wait until there were just two of them alone. He would come home and terrorize them. Then he figured out that two of them could take him. So, he would wait until there was just one. He could come home and terrorize them—beat them up.

We all pretended like nothing was going on. Violence was not something that you talked about in the 60's. Bev hid from him a lot. She hid in her bedroom.

I didn't feel very good about myself. By the time I was 12 I kept hearing how dumb I was from my brothers and my dad. They said I couldn't do anything right. I started believing it.

**I am in fourth grade. Maybe you can see my mischievous spirt starting to show itself.**

Dad treated me different than he treated the other brothers. For example, we went through fire arm safety class when we were in fourth or fifth grade. He bought each of the other brothers a 22 after they passed the fire arm safety class. But when I went through fire arm safety, he didn't buy me one. Nothing was ever said about it. Of course, I was expecting to get my own 22 just like my brothers. I didn't say anything but my feelings were hurt bad.

Dad seemed to want to make a show of his boys entering manhood. He gave each of my brothers a razor and shaving cream as soon as they got old enough to shave—first Bill, then Bruce, Bob and Bud. But again when it came my turn, he didn't give me a razor. Again he didn't say anything.

It bothered me. Why was he excluding me? I sensed that somehow he was disowning me or acting like I didn't belong to him. I didn't like the feeling. It was always in the background in my relationship with him. He doesn't think I quite fit it. After a while I came to believe that I didn't fit in—that I didn't belong.

Nothing was ever said, but everyone in the family was aware that Dad treated me in a different way. I later learned the dark secret.

When I was born my mom and dad were separated. They had been together nine months earlier when I was conceived, but when Dad returned home, he found out that he had another son. My mother told me later that he was angry and accused her of having an affair with a truck driver. He said that he didn't believe that I was his son.

So, for all my growing up years he usually treated me like someone who didn't really belong to the family.

In the spring of 1971, Bill, my oldest brother, had a terrible motorcycle accident. He was transferred to Fargo to the biggest hospital around. He had a severe head injury. The doctors said nothing could be done.

I was 11 at the time, and I was terrified. Mom and I spent most of that summer in Fargo with Bill. I remember coming home one week without Mom. Bruce, Bob, Bud and Dad had no clean clothes. So I took it upon myself to do the laundry. We had an old wringer washer with rinse tubs. I hung the clothes on a line in the backyard.

That's when things started getting bad. Mom and I were in Fargo. The brothers were running the garbage route. Dad was working—driving trucks and doing whatever. Bruce was 16 that summer and he ran away. I didn't know it at the time, but the old man was beating all three of my brothers at home—Bruce, Bob and Bud.

### THE FIGHT

Finally Bill got home from the hospital. He had brain damage, and he was down to 110 pounds. One night all hell broke loose. I remember Bud and Bob and Dad on the dining room floor fighting. They were punching and wrestling—Bud and Bob against my dad. Bill was standing there screaming in terror. Mom is screaming and trying to stop the fighting. I ran out the door screaming, "I'm getting the cops." I got to the road and fell to the ground bawling.

That night I decided never to let anyone make me feel that way again. That night was the end of innocence. I started to drink.

# 2

# Drunk at 12

## The first time I got drunk

The first time I got drunk would have been January of '72. I came home, and my brothers Bob and Bud, a guy named Turtle Mountain Ray, and Larry Braulick were sitting around the kitchen drinking Hot Toddies. I didn't know what they were drinking or what it tasted like, so they gave me one. Then they gave me another one.

Mom wasn't home. She was working at the nursing home. Dad, Bill and Bruce were someplace else. I don't know where they were.

I liked it. I liked the taste—brandy and water and sugar or honey. Those drinks tasted good, and they went down smooth. I started getting this warm sensation. They gave me another one, and I felt even better. Then Bev walked in – Bev and her husband. There we were drinking. She didn't say much about Bud and Bob drinking but she was really upset with me. She saw Turtle Mountain Ray there. She knew that he had supplied the alcohol. Bob, Bud and I were only 15, 14 and 12. Turtle Mountain Ray was a Native American. He was staying in McIntosh at that time. We called him Turtle Mountain Ray because he came from the Turtle Mountain Reservation. He was a big old fat guy. He'd buy booze for underage kids and help them drink it. We had a number of people doing that in McIntosh when we were kids.

That night after Bev left we decided we'd ride around with Danny Salvaus. I remember feeling like I was one of the boys. There was a real comradery. I was having fun with my brothers until I got sick. I was sitting in the back seat, right behind the driver, and I spewed puke all over the back of his head. I remember doing that—distinctly.

Then the door opened, and I rolled out into the ditch. It was January, and I rolled into a snowbank. They decided to take me home. I remember Bud taking me into the house and putting me in bed in the top bunk. That was the last thing I remember until Mom found me lying between her bed and the wall. I somehow got downstairs from my bedroom into Mom and Dad's bedroom. I was lying on the floor, and there was Mom waking me up.

**My sixth grade photo**

I blacked out the very first time I got drunk. A black out—if you don't know what it is—you're functioning physically but mentally you don't know what you are doing. So there's a blank space in your life. You don't know what has happened during that time until someone tells you.

My mom was very, very upset. She said, "What if your dad gets home now? What are we going to do when your dad gets home?" She brought me in the kitchen and gave me a cup of coffee. I tried drinking that coffee, and once again I spewed all over the kitchen table. Mom cleaned that up and got me in bed.

The next day I was extremely hung over. I had a headache like

I'd never had before. I think I drank a pint that first time—a pint of brandy. It was probably four or five mixed drinks. That's how I got so drunk and blacked out. The next day I woke up and I was sick. Oh! I could hardly move, it hurt so bad.

Everyone was going out to visit some friends in the country—play cards and what not. But I stayed at home on the couch. I was too sick to go. At that point I said, "I'm never going to do this again." And I didn't for a while. But my brothers drank. My dad drank. Everybody around me drank except Mom and Bev. My brothers drank to get drunk. My dad drank to get drunk. There was never social drinking. Mom would have a beer once in a while but very rarely. Bev hardly drank at all. Excessive drinking seems to affect only the males in my family.

While I was still 12 years old Mom and Dad bought a restaurant in Fosston. Mom ran it. For a while we lived in a small apartment in Fosston with Mom. There were two bedrooms, and there were four of us in there. Bruce was home, Bud was home, Bob was home. We had two bedrooms and a couch. At that time Mom was trying to be the opposite of my father, and she tried too hard. She was lenient on us. She thought she was doing the right thing. It had been so bad for so long, she thought she'd lighten up.

#### I start smoking weed

That is when I first smoked weed. The first time, Bobby and Chad offered it to me—Bobby Finkle and Chad Burslie. Bobby was in my same grade, and Chad was a grade ahead of us. I was still playing with toy trucks in the driveway. I was still a little boy. I was 12 but I was very immature.

At that time I smoked a cigarette once in a while. They were my mom's Raleigh filters. We were up by Tammy Youmans' place. They invited me up there and offered me some weed. They said they were going to get me stoned. I freaked out and left. I didn't touch it. But about six weeks later Bruce showed up. He asked me,

"You wanna smoke some pot?"

"Yeah." I said. This was my big brother. He was sort of my hero. If he smoked weed, it was OK. In fact, I wanted to imitate him.

We were standing behind the rec center in Fosston smoking a little weed. No big deal. I didn't get stoned that time. Then Bruce went into the army. About that time a friend of Bud's called looking for him. When I explained that Bud wasn't home, he asked, "Do you smoke pot?"

**Chad Burslie**

Of course, I was this tough kid. I said, "Yeah, I smoke it all the time." So he invited me to come smoke with him. Greg Woods, a kid from Fosston, was with me. We joined him down by the municipal water plant. The three of us sat behind there and started smoking Columbian Red. I smoked a bowl and they said, "You get high?"

"No. I don't feel any different."

We smoked another bowl (a pipe full of pot). After that second pipeful, they asked, "You high?"

"No. I don't feel any different." We were passing this pipe around. Finally, he filled a third bowl. We smoked some more, and he said, "Are you high yet?"

I said, "I don't think so. I don't feel any different." Then I stood up and fell right over. I was really, really high. I fell in love with pot. The first time I got stoned, I said, " I like this. This makes me happy. It makes me laugh. It helps me relax."

It took me a half hour to walk three blocks to get home. Everything seemed real funny. We finally reached the pool hall, and I just sat there and giggled. I didn't do anything else. I just sat there and giggled. That was my first experience with getting stoned.

I giggled all the way home. It never got me sick. I took to weed like a fish to water. I liked it right from the get-go. It relaxed me. I could laugh at things.

#### Getting drunk the second time

I don't remember the circumstances of drinking the second time. It was just there. I don't remember what happened, but something happened and once again I drank to get drunk. I liked drinking. I liked the taste, and I liked the feeling. I liked the taste of beer from the first time I sipped it from my father's Hamm's beer can.

Getting so sick on my first drunk made me not want to drink again. I'm sure I didn't drink again for at least six months. I was still this little boy, playing in the driveway with my toy cars and trucks. Now I was drinking, and I was turning into another guy. I tried to keep my drinking a secret from Mom and Bev, but my brothers all knew I drank.

After I started drinking my circle of friends changed. Kevin moved away from me when I started drinking. Terry Strom was a really good friend. He was a couple of years younger than me. We used to play together all the time, and he just disappeared out of sight.

**My friend Jelly Roll**

Other guys replaced them—Danny Bak and Jelly Roll. They drank. Jelly Roll was more into weed, but he would drink sometimes. And Bobby Finkle. We were all 12-13 year olds. We're all drinking and smoking pot. It was the 70's.

Bruce ran away. Then Bud ran away. They ran away in 1972

or 73. They would come and go. Bruce was the first to go. He hitchhiked down to Florida. Then Bud ran away. Bud was really young when he ran away—about 14. He ran away to California and Florida. I don't know for sure what they did and how they lived. I suppose they were homeless.

It was probably early in 1973 when I was still 13, Bob and I were the only children left at home with our mother. My mom and I were in the living room watching TV, when Bob walked in. I could tell that he had had a few drinks. He announced, "I can't take it no more, Mom. I can't take it no more. I'm not going to let him beat me up again." He got the 12 gauge and loaded it. He stood there with the loaded 12 gauge pointed at the front door. If Dad had walked in, Bob would have shot him.

Mom and I talked to him, talked to him, talked to him. Finally, we called my sister Bev who lived a mile out in the country with her husband. She came and got him out of there so that he wouldn't kill Dad.

Probably he had gotten beat up the previous day when he was the only one at home and he couldn't defend himself. Dad was a big man, and Bob was only 15 years old at the time.

Bob stayed overnight with Bev and her husband, and he came back the next day. The effect of that on me was that I resolved that I really, really didn't like my father. I realized the severity of violence in my life, and my father was the cause of all this violence in my family. Up until that point I had been able to push off the violence and hide it. But now I hated the domestic violence. Now with my brother standing there ready to kill him, it hit me that all this violence was very real in my life. I was going through puberty at that time. I was struggling with that. My emotions were everywhere. I didn't want to be with Dad, but I didn't want to be with my brothers and Mom. I hated what was going on in my life, and I started hiding more in the alcohol. I think that is when my drinking really, really took off.

### Mom leaves Dad

I was both proud and ashamed of myself at the same time. I had a sense of freedom—especially after Mom left Dad. It must have been late '72, early '73. The violence was really bad. He was beating both her and us.

Mom took Bob, Bud and Bill, and they all went to International Falls, but I wouldn't go with them. I don't know exactly why I didn't go with them. I think I wanted to keep the family together. I knew the family was falling apart. So, I stayed home with Dad. I remember Dad and I going to the truck stop to have dinner and he said, "Well, my oldest boy is no longer a man. And the rest of them all run off on me. I guess that makes you the number one son." I suppose that made me feel good at the time. I think I always wanted the love and respect of my father. It kind of made me feel special that I was with Dad. I was trying to keep things together. It was a confusing time for me. I wanted my father's love and respect, and at the same time I hated my father and the violence he carried with him. That is probably the key turning point—when Mom left and the real violence had set in—and Bob standing there with that 12 gauge.

We moved out, actually. We moved out of the house into Paul's grandma's house. Paul Aakhus was married to my sister, Bev. Paul's grandmother died and left this little house. Mom rented it. I remember the stairs to the second floor were so steep, they were just like a ladder. It was a little place. My mother moved into this house. Paul and Bev were still out in the country. It was Mom and her boys. So we were living in the same town with our father who continued living in our old house. Now he was there all by himself. Bill would be back and forth between Mom and Dad. I was in eighth grade at the time. So, I would have been 13.

There was such a big stink about our hair and our drinking, Mom thought if we were going to drink, it was better that we drank at home. I remember the first time that Mom bought beer for my older brothers. One of my brothers said something. They must have been teasing me. I forget the exact details, but I remember that I blew up. I was in such a state of confusion. There was so much hurt in my life. I recognize now how emotionally unstable I was. My emotions were everywhere.

All it took was one spark, and I exploded. One of my brothers said something to me, and I said, "Fuck you" right in front of my mom. I was thirteen years old. They realized that I was starting to lose it. So they sent me to Grand Forks to live with my cousin and aunt for a while to get me out of McIntosh. Shortly after that we moved to Fosston for the restaurant.

I was making wine when I was thirteen years old, and Mom knew it. You take Welch's grape juice, a bunch of sugar and a bunch of yeast. You mix it all up, and you set it in the corner of your closet for a month, six weeks. Then you skim off the rotten stuff and drink the rest.

### Mom gets a divorce and the house

That summer Mom took Dad to court. She got a divorce, and she got the house. So, Dad moved out, and we moved back to the McIntosh house. Now they were divorced. For years they were off and on. They would break up, and then they'd get back together. Mom finally got the divorce in 1973, and they never got remarried after that. They would live together at times, but they were no longer married.

After Mom left Dad I worked in the CETA program. I can't remember what the initials stood for. It was a program for low income kids to work at the school during the summer. We worked 32 hours a week, and we were paid minimum wage – that was $1.60 an hour in those days. I started doing that at 13. I kept that CETA job until I was 15, so I always had spending money.

One of my good drinking buddies was Danny Bak, Danny's mom would go to the liquor store and buy us a six pack. She was Native American. She supplied it to us, and we paid for it. I always had money. Each of us would drink three cans of beer, and we would get a very good buzz from that. Then my tolerance started growing. I started with Danny when I was thirteen, and by the time I was fifteen I could drink a case of beer by myself. I was proud of my tolerance. I could outdrink most people my age as well as a lot of people older than me.

### I go to jail

We began to break into the school in Fosston to play on the trampoline. We did this pretty much every Sunday. We'd take a pocket knife and open up the gym door. One time there were seven of us in there, and some of the guys broke into the pop machine. We all had free pop. We broke into the kitchen and helped ourselves to ice cream. The next thing you know we were running around chasing each other with fire extinguishers and tearing up the school. Somebody poured pop in the typewriters. But we got caught by a teacher. It was Sunday, and she just happened to come to school for something that day.

When we got caught, we knew we were in trouble. So, we took off and went to Roy Lake on the Indian reservation. The dad of a friend of ours had a cabin there. We stayed there for two or three days. We were hiding out, eating whatever we could find to eat. At one point I cooked crayfish in a coffee can.

Everybody else wanted to go back, and I didn't want to go back. "Naw, let's stay here. We can figure out how to eat."

They said, "No. No. We gotta go back. We gotta go back."

We got halfway back to Fosston, and the cops picked us up. I was probably thirteen. I actually went to jail that day for a few hours.

When I was fourteen, I was confirmed into the Lutheran church. I had been baptized in a Methodist Church, and now I was getting confirmed into a Lutheran church. I called myself a "Methadran."

I never went to the confirmation classes. I didn't do the study work they wanted me to do. I never learned the chapters of the Bible. I was pretty angry. I had a real authority problem. For the final step we were examined by the church leaders. We stood there, and they asked us questions. I didn't know the answers to any of them. The teacher finally phrased the questions, so that the answer was always, "God." That got me through the confirmation test.

**In 1973, at age 14, I got confirmed**

At that time Mom was sick, so Dad came with me. I had smoked pot and inhaled paint thinner that morning before I went to church and was confirmed. That was also the last time I went to church. Now that I was confirmed, it meant the end of my church going.

When I was drinking, I didn't feel bad. My feelings were numbed. I could go out and have fun. I could hang out with my buddies, especially with Danny Bak and his mom.

I definitely started spending more time away from home. I would be gone as much as I could. I would be at my friends' place—mostly Danny Bak. Then there was Jelly Roll. Danny and I had a disagreement about drinking. So I started spending more time with Jelly Roll who smoked pot, and Bobby Finkle who smoked pot and drank.

When I was in ninth grade, there were thirteen of us on an eleven-man football team and ten of us drank and smoked weed. It was really prevalent—the drugs and alcohol.

I started doing White Cross amphetamine pills at fourteen. Most of my friends were older than me because of my brothers. I was the youngest Fritz boy. I was just accepted by these older guys. They were three to five years older than me. They gave me access to drugs and booze.

### MY FIFTEENTH BIRTHDAY PARTY AND THE MAGIC OF LSD

My fifteenth birthday was coming up on August 1, 1974. I saved up a little money to celebrate. I guess I could have hosted a birthday party for myself with cokes and hot dogs and a big chocolate cake with 15 candles, but I wasn't interested in that sort of party.

It was Friday night, and I bought a bunch of beer. I went driving around with Larry Braulick, John Defrank and Bobby Finkle. We ended up down in Winger—about 13 miles south of McIntosh. We were drinking and getting pretty drunk.

There was this Volkswagen sitting there up on blocks. It was owned by one of the town drunks, and some guys had lifted it unto some blocks so the tires were just off the ground. He would get in the car, start it up and give it gas, and the wheels would just spin. In our infinite wisdom we lifted that car up off the blocks, rolled it toward a cliff and then pushed it over the cliff so it crashed. Nobody could see if for days.

It got wrecked, we got caught, and we wound up having to buy that Volkswagen. Later that night we ran into David and Arnold Qualley, and they said, "Let's have a beer." The bartender looked at me sort of sideways and Arnold said, "It's his birthday today. He just turned 18."

The drinking age was 18 at that time. So the guy served me. That gave me the confidence that I could drink in a bar. That was an important step for me.

Anyway Friday night was my birthday. We drank and drove around all day Saturday. We went down to the pavilion in Maple Lake. There was a dance every Sunday night in the summer. We went down there, and we were drinking pretty heavily and smoking weed. We ran into David Qualley. I hadn't seen him in a while.

David asked me, "Hey, you wanna do some acid?"

I said "UH?"

He explained, "LSD. I got some really good stuff. I'll give it to you for two bucks."

So we bought this hit of acid. We broke it into three pieces for Larry, Bobby and me. We each took a piece of it. I stuck the piece in my mouth like a piece of candy, chewed a little and swallowed.

Anyway when I took this acid we were driving back to Winger and the world started moving. The world started to vibrate. I would move my hand, and I would see a hundred hands trailing along behind. Everything seemed more intense—the colors and everything. I really, really liked it. It took me completely out of reality. It made everything different. Cars would disappear. Trees would move. It was so extreme.

Larry was driving, but when we got to Winger we thought we shouldn't keep driving. We started walking around. When we got to the liquor store, it started to move a little bit. We freaked out.

The LSD cost only two bucks, and three of us got high on it. It was a really fun night. I loved LSD. I loved it. The more I did it, the more I liked it.

After my fifteenth birthday, I learned that I could buy my own booze. I could sit in the bar in numerous different places. It made it a lot easier. All I had to do was go over to Erskine and buy my beer. I always had money. I worked. From when I was thirteen until I was fifteen, I worked regular hours at CETA each summer. I had spending money.

Once I was fifteen I started disappearing for three or four days at a time. Mom couldn't control me. I did what John wanted to do. I was fifteen, and I didn't answer to anybody.

Then I got busted for marijuana when I was fifteen. I was the first person in McIntosh to get busted for drugs. It was Prom Night. I was with Bobby Finkle and Timmy Anderson and Tony, we were all driving around in Bud's car. He was in the Navy, and I had his car. I didn't have a driver's license so

I had Bobby drive it. We had all sorts of alcohol in the car. We were going to go to the Teen Scene to play some pool. We were waiting for the real Prom Party to start. We pulled up to the Teen Scene. It was a teen hangout place. When we pulled up there, the cops were sitting there. We all started bailing out. They stuck their heads in, and they asked if Durocher was there, and I said, "No, he's not."

"Well, we need to talk to you."

I got out of the car. I had an army field jacket, and there was a bag of pot sticking out of my pocket. We were so careful to hide all the booze. But we never thought about the drugs.

They searched the car and found all sorts of homemade water pipes. They reached over and said, "What's this?"

I said, "Oh, it looks like a half ounce." What more could I say? They wrote me up and then sent me home. At that time when people would ask me how I could carry on despite being drunk or high, I would say, "It's no big deal. I'm not playing a piano." That is what I always said. I thought it was a clever response.

The next morning my mom found out that I had been busted for marijuana. They didn't throw me in jail because I was a juvenile, but I had to go to court. I was only 15. I went to court, and they put me on probation for two years. That didn't stop me from drinking or smoking weed or anything like that. I just kept doing it.

### I am arrested for breaking and entering

I had just turned sixteen, and I got caught breaking and entering into the 3.2 joint. I used to go in there, almost every Sunday night when it was closed. I would take two cases of beer, a half a dozen packs of cigarettes, a few bags of potato chips and maybe $10 in change. I'd just steal it. I went in there every week or two for a year. I would crawl in the bathroom window, and I'd go out the back door and leave that door unlocked. It looked like one of the employees forgot to lock up. I got by with this for a long time.

Then my brother Bud brought one of his Navy buddies home on leave. I told this guy about my clever arrangement. He went in and rifled the place, took all the money and made a mess of things. He ruined my gig.

The next morning I told my brother Bill the whole story. He turned me in. I was ashamed. That was the last time I ever stole anything.

**A photo taken just after my sixteenth birthday**

It was the fall of 1975. I had turned sixteen, and I was kept in jail for eleven days. Mom and Dad were trying to patch things up, and they went on vacation with each other. That's when I did the breaking and entering at Sylvia's 3.2 bar. I wound up in a jail cell with padded walls in the Polk County Jail. They put me into solitary confinement.

Everybody in my family knew I was there. My breaking into Sylvia's was big news. In a town of 800 people when somebody breaks into something, it's big news. Bud did come and see me. They wouldn't let him in because he was a juvenile—not quite eighteen. So, he handed the deputy a pack of cigarettes and said, "At least give my little brother these."

Well, he brought me up this pack of cigarettes. I started smoking them, and all of a sudden joints started falling out. So I was sitting there smoking marijuana cigarettes in the jail. They left me alone in this cell for eleven days. Mom and Dad were in Arizona. The rest of the family thought I deserved to be there—including Bev.

After eleven days my mind was really wondering, "What the

hell! Doesn't anybody care?" Finally, the pastor of our church, came and got me. He talked Bev into taking me in.

### Mom wants me to go to chemical treatment

I was sixteen. I was already on probation for the marijuana, and now I was also on probation for breaking and entering. I was in and out of home. Mom and Dad got back together, and I left. I didn't want to be there. I would go stay with Danny Bak or Jelly Roll or the cabin in the park. That spring they would pick me up and take me into juvenile hall (it was a place to keep troubled juveniles) and then send me home. Within a week I would leave home again. I didn't want to be there. Some days, as soon as I got home, I would leave that same day.

Finally in that summer before my seventeenth birthday, Mom wanted me to try a treatment center. It happened like this: I was hitch hiking from Fosston trying to get back to McIntosh. My probation officer pulled over. I jumped into his car.

He said, "What are you doing? Your mom said you ran away."

"I didn't run away. I'm just not staying there anymore. I don't want to be there anymore. But I'm still around."

He said, "Well, your mom thinks you've got an alcohol and drug problem. I'll make a deal with you. You go into Glenmore Treatment center in Crookston for an evaluation, and we'll see what happens. You have to follow their recommendation."

So, I went to Glenmore. They did all sorts of evaluation on me. I took the MMPI (Minnesota Multiphasic Personality Inventory) and all sorts of stuff. I was there for eight or nine days. During that time I went to my first AA meeting just for something to do. I was sixteen. The AA meeting was all a bunch of older people.

I knew I had a drinking problem. So I made up my mind that I wasn't going to drink anymore. I was just going to do drugs. But I just went back to drinking again. That made me realize that I had both a drinking problem and drug problem, because I had tried to quit without success. But in the treatment center I didn't tell them the truth about anything. I made up stories and I guess they believed me.

The drug counselors said, "Well, we've come to the conclusion that you don't have a problem with alcohol and drugs. You are a very intelligent sixteen-year-old, smart ass." They came to the conclusion that I didn't need treatment.

The probation officer said, "I'll see to it that you don't have to go back to your dad." They took me into court and emancipated me. Technically that wasn't legal in Minnesota, but my parents didn't know that.

Beginning when I was twelve and got drunk for the first time, my life had begun to fall apart. The violence and trouble in my family pushed me into drinking and drugging. At first I drank and did drugs to numb the pain of my life. But then I started becoming addicted to drinking and drugs, and my life fell apart even more.

I had troubles at other stages in my life when my life seemed to unravel, but in this period from the time I was twelve until I was sixteen, I seemed helpless as I watched my life coming apart. I was a little boy when I was twelve. I was small for my age, and I was immature. I still liked to play with my toy trucks in our driveway. At age twelve I was a pretty innocent boy who sipped a little beer, but I had never been drunk and never done drugs of any kind. By the end of this period at age sixteen, I was getting drunk, getting stoned, buying and selling weed, getting arrested for drugs and breaking and entering. I was on the edge—about to become homeless. It seemed that everything changed in those years between twelve and sixteen.

### What is next for me?

It was hard to imagine what was next for me. Most of my brothers had already run away from home and were now in the (military) service. I was still at home, but I was getting into trouble. I hated my father and wanted to get away from him. I had finished my junior year of high school, but I didn't like school. But I was only sixteen. What next?

# 3

# Homeless at Sixteen

## Living in the log cabin in McIntosh

I didn't know what to do. It was the beginning of the summer of 1976. I was 16, and I didn't want to live at home any more. So, I decided to move out—just like all of my brothers had done. I was still in school. The only place I really knew was McIntosh. So I decided to get away from the house and away from my father and find someplace else to sleep.

There was a nice little park in McIntosh. In that park there was a log cabin and a brick building with showers that had been built the year before. There was a toilet connected to the shower room. When I first moved into the cabin the doors and windows had all been ripped off. But it was a solidly built—going back to the 1940's. There was no electricity, so it was mostly dark at night except for a street light. The door that was ripped off was lying on the floor, so I used that as a bed to keep me off the concrete. I left my sleeping bag, a change of clothes and all my stuff right there in the cabin. Nobody bothered anything.

I just used the cabin for sleeping. One night I returned to the cabin, and someone had left four beers there for me. I was tickled pink. But nobody ever bothered me. There I was—a 16-year-old boy living in a log cabin in the town park. Nobody seemed to know or care what I was doing.

**I moved into this log cabin when I was 16**

It was quiet there—real quiet at night time. During the day I would hitchhike to Lengby Lake or Fosston, Crookston or Grand Forks, just for something to do. I thought maybe I could find some drugs or alcohol.

I cleaned my clothes by going swimming in them. I went down to Lengby Lake and went swimming with my clothes on. I had some shampoo, and I washed my hair and washed my clothes at the same time. I let nature dry me off.

For eating I mostly went over to see Danny Bak. I also worked for my brother Bill who was then running the family garbage business. I earned a few bucks.

Of course I was drinking all the time—wherever I could find a drink. I went over to Danny's house where there was always something to drink. My brother Bill would buy me booze when I worked for him. Sometimes the beer was warm, but I didn't care. If it was alcohol, I drank it.

The biggest challenge each day was getting something to eat. The next challenge was—how can I get drunk? I always wanted to get drunk. If I had a few drinks, but not enough to get drunk,

**I was in 10th grade in 1974**

I was disappointed. I was never one to say, "Let's go have a beer." I said, "Let's go get drunk." There were a few inconveniences, like trying to stay dry. When it rained, I just stayed inside the cabin. But mostly I was so happy to be free. On a scale of one to ten, my happiness was at an "8." I was doing what I wanted to do. I was removed from violence. After years of violence and terror, being emancipated gave me a sense of freedom. I didn't have to answer to anybody. I could take care of myself and do what I damn well pleased. It was relief.

### I QUIT SCHOOL

My senior year began in September of 1976. I woke up in the log cabin and went to the first day of class for my senior year. But I didn't get the classes that I wanted. I realized that I wouldn't graduate because of the lack of credits. So, I decided I didn't want to go to school. I decided I had better things to do. School got in the way of my partying.

By now I had become an outcast in my own hometown. In a town of 800 my drinking and my arrests had become well known. Everyone told their daughters to "stay away from that Fritz boy." I couldn't date any of the girls in town. I was an outcast.

### I FIND A JOB IN CROOKSTON

I turned 17 that summer, and I went down to Crookston looking for a job. I applied for a job at the American Crystal Sugar Company sugar beet factory. They said, "Well, you can hang around

**The American Crystal Sugar plant in Crookston, Minnesota**

here until four this afternoon when the shift changes, and if we need anybody, we'll know by five."

I met a guy named Kenny Williams from California. He was looking for work, too. We both came back at 4 o'clock, and they said, "We don't need you. Come back at 11."

We went to the bar, and we stayed in the bar until 10:30. Now I was really drunk. I went back to the American Crystal Sugar Company with Kenny, and they hired us. They gave us some simple work to do so we could sober up. They sent Kenny to one area of the plant and me to another. I was leaning on a broom for a couple of hours before I started stacking 100-pound bags of sugar. There were three of us stacking these bags of sugar in huge stacks. I started sweating that booze out. I sobered up.

When our shift was over, Kenny and I got together again. Kenny told me about a three-bedroom, one-bath house that we could rent. We moved in.

I began spending a lot of time in the bar after work. At work I was assigned to run a pulverizer to make powdered sugar and bag it into 100-pound bags. I had the night shift. We manufactured about three tons every night. I was paid $3.65 an hour which was pretty good money.

### My first girlfriend

One night shortly after Kenny and I got jobs at American Crystal Sugar, we went to the Viking Bar in downtown Crookston to hang out. Sitting at the bar were two girls. Kenney was in his early 30's at the time, and he said, "Let's dance with them." He had a lot more experience with girls than I did.

When I was in high school I wasn't very successful with girls. I was scared of them. Well, we started dancing. We later learned they were cousins—Janet and Donna. Janet was 18 at the time. I was dancing with Janet, but she had too much to drink and was feeling sick, so we went outside. We sat there together talking. She liked the fact that I didn't hit on her, but just sat with her and talked. She thought I was a true gentleman. We exchanged phone numbers. She showed interest in me. In fact, she phoned me the next day. She asked if I wanted to get together, and I said, "Of course." She came over to my place. She was living with her folks at the time, and her mom was an alcoholic, so she started coming over to my place on a regular basis. Janet was a very attractive girl. She had dark hair and dark eyes. She was small. She had a sweet little voice. I had never really had a girlfriend. She was kind of shy. She was new to the party scene. I was only 17 but I had been going to bars for two years already. I found Janet irresistible right away. I really wanted to be with her.

**Janet was my first girlfriend**

When she came over to the house, we watched TV. We listened to a lot of music. In those days I liked "Kiss" and "Black Sabbath" and "Pink Floyd"—all hard rock and roll. I don't know if she really liked it or just put up with it for me.

The next thing you know, we were dating. Well, she was still pretty shy. I think I was the first fellow she slept with. I was her first, and she was my second. She was nervous, and didn't know exactly what to do. Her cousin Donna explained what to do. She wasn't very sexual at first. But soon she became very sexual and very active. I could sleep with her whenever I wanted to. She had a good job. She worked in a jewelry store. She really liked jewelry. So I bought her a diamond for Christmas in 1976. I really, really liked her.

I was pretty happy. I felt really good about myself. I was able to shower every day and keep myself clean. I wanted to keep myself clean to impress this girl. Here is somebody who liked me, who wanted to be with me. I had a house, a decent job, a great girlfriend. Life was good.

I was mostly drinking beer in those days. In a typical day I would drink 18 to 24 cans of beer. My capacity for alcohol had increased a lot since my first drunk at age 12. Now it took a full case of beer for me to get happily drunk. I didn't drink on the job. I waited until I got off work. I was very proud of that.

I would get up in the morning and skip breakfast. I had a charge account at the café of the sugar plant. So I charged my lunch. Then I came home. For dinner I drank and maybe ate a few potatoes. On weekends we really drank. Then we drank whiskey with our beer.

### I TRY TO QUIT DRINKING

By this time I had tried to quit drinking several times. I knew drinking was causing me problems. I had a decent job. I had a house. I had a wonderful girlfriend. If I could just quit drinking,

I could begin to have a good life. But I didn't quit. At some point we got down to a 50-pound bag of potatoes and three jars of mayonnaise in the fridge. I decided I had to do something different. This wasn't working well. I was spending all my money on booze.

In December of 1976 I realized that something had to change. I didn't have food in my house. I was having trouble paying my share of the rent. My brothers had been in military service. Bruce, Bob and Bud had all been in the service – two in the Army and one in the Navy. I decided I would go in the Navy and make a career of it. It just sounded like a good idea.

I would have a paycheck every two weeks. I would have food and everything I needed. It was a Sunday night, and I was drinking with two buddies in Red Lake Falls at the only bar that was open. I decided that night that I was going into the Navy. I would go into the Navy and retire after 20 years. I would be only 37 years old and have a nice pension. It sounded like a really, really good idea. I was excited about it.

Of course, it was always in the back of my mind that I could quit if I didn't like it. Bud did a tour in Vietnam. He was in the final evacuation. After his service in Vietnam, he quit.

## I Join the Navy

I knew that if I wasn't going to be around, I had to break up with Janet. No sense in my trying to keep a girlfriend in Minnesota when I was going to be stationed in California. So I broke up with her.

I figured I would go to boot camp and everything would be wonderful. I would go to San Diego and get transferred to a nice ship, like my brother was on. I wanted anti-submarine service, but they put me in aviation fire control on the Kitty Hawk, a big aircraft carrier. I had no clue what fire control was.

I was assigned to boot camp in Chicago in January. Physically it wasn't that hard, but mentally it was hard. They liked to mess with you mentally. Once I was in boot camp, I realized that I made a mistake. I had people telling me what to do. I had this "authority problem." I wasn't able to drink during boot camp, but I smoked a lot of pot. There was a guy from Chicago in my unit, and he told this other guy how to get some pot. We had a lot of pot brought to us.

**In my Navy uniform**

I started getting into trouble. I went "UA"—unauthorized absence. Then they gave me a court martial with 10 days in the brig and took two-thirds of my pay. The brig wasn't so bad. It was just another jail. No big deal.

I was 17 years old, cock of the walk, ten feet tall and bulletproof. After ten days in the brig, they shipped me off to San Diego to serve on an aircraft carrier. I didn't want to be on an aircraft carrier. I wanted anti-submarine warfare so I could be on a battleship. But here I was in training for aircraft fire control technician. I didn't last long.

I was stationed in Millington, Tennessee. And I didn't like it. I didn't like the Navy. I went UA again. This time I went back up to McIntosh for high school graduation. My classmates were now seniors, and they were graduating from high school. They were the boys and girls I had grown up with.

They had the graduation in the McIntosh High School gym. I stood just inside the backdoor of the gym and watched the graduation ceremony. All my old classmates were dressed in gowns, and they were marching up to the stage to receive their diploma and shake hands. I watched it all.

I almost cried. I was really, really depressed. I wasn't there graduating with them. I felt like I didn't belong. I felt like I was a forgotten person—like nobody missed me and nobody cared. Just before the ceremony ended, I left and went to the bar. I sat in the bar by myself the rest of the night. I didn't go to the graduation parties or anything.

I stayed in McIntosh a couple days. I didn't see any of my friends. Then I took off for California. I had a lot of emotions—guilt, shame, depression. Here I am in the Navy, and I can't deal with that. Where am I going? What am I doing with my life?

I had been UA again. So, I went back to California and turned myself in to the Navy. Maybe the only thing I liked about the Navy was the drugs. It was 1977, and drugs were everywhere, especially in California. Drinking was more of a problem. I remember the first time I went to a bar. They wouldn't let me in because I was only 17 years old. I said, "Here I am in the military, serving my country and you don't serve me a beer?" I blew up big time over that. But I could drink on the base. We had a bar called the Ratskeller.

Because of my latest unauthorized absence, they put me in the "restriction barracks." One day a Navy lawyer came to me and said they were going to send me back to San Diego. I explained that if they sent me back to the Kitty Hawk, I would leave again. I asked if they would assign me to a different ship. He said they couldn't do that. Then he asked, "Would you like a discharge?" I said "Sure. Will you give me an honorable discharge?" He said he could give me a "General discharge under honorable conditions." I took it.

### Back with Janet and then I disappear again

I returned to northern Minnesota, and I resumed my relationship with Janet. We picked up where we left off. It was now 1978. Things were going along really well. All of the sudden I realized that she was pregnant. It scared me, terrified me. She didn't tell me and I didn't ask. It was "Don't ask; don't tell." But I could see she was pregnant

I knew she was pregnant. We had been together close to a year. I didn't say anything to her or anybody clsc. I got my backpack, and I just disappeared one day. Although I wanted to be a father, I wasn't ready to be a father at that time. I knew that. Once I was out in California, I thought about Janet a lot. But I never contacted her. I didn't write to her or phone her. I never contacted my family either.

I was just living on the streets in California, doing drugs and drinking. I didn't have a job. I didn't have a place to live. That's when I really learned to be homeless in a big city. I went from this town of 800 people to San Diego, California—living on the streets. It was much more dangerous.

About a year later I returned to northern Minnesota, and Janet's cousin told me that she had been having physical problems with her pregnancy, and it was terminated. I don't know if the part about "physical problems" was true or not. But it really bothered me. I had to recognize that she had an abortion. I didn't believe in abortions. I didn't think it should be used as a form of birth control.

Now I recognized that there was a little wedge pushing us apart—not only me taking off to California but now the abortion. Somehow we got back together. We never talked about the baby or the abortion. We just put it on the shelf and pretended it didn't happen. We got back together off and on until I was 19. I had been living in McIntosh, but then I disappeared again.

### Wandering around like a stray dog

I would stay around for a month or two, and then I would disappear. I hitchhiked coast to coast along Interstate 40 and sometimes Interstate 20 back and forth a half dozen times that year. I had no place to go. It was too cold to be up north. I just kept wandering around like a stray dog with no place to go.

I was hitchhiking full time. That is when I learned to become a chameleon. I could be what people wanted me to be. When I was hitchhiking, I could get into a car, and I could read somebody. If the driver was a Christian, I could read that. Then I would talk Christianity with them. If they were a party person, I could talk partying with them. I could tell them a story that they wanted to hear—in order to get money out of them.

I made up stories that would appeal to that particular person. Sometimes I was a married guy who got kicked out of his house by his wife and the kids. Sometimes I was a runaway from home when I was real young, and I had never been home since. Sometimes I was trying to get home for holidays. It all depended upon the type of person I was riding with.

Sometimes I got rides from guys who wanted sex. I remember the first time a guy said, "I'll give you twenty five bucks to let me suck your dick." I needed twenty five bucks, so I said OK. We did it right in the car. It was really, really hard that first time. It bothered me a lot. I felt guilty. I felt ashamed. But the next time somebody offered, it was easier. It got easier and easier and easier. Hitch hikers called it "survival sex." It was pretty common.

I got to where I was really, really good at getting money out of people. People were generous. I have always been lucky with people being generous with me. It was a combination of generous people and my skill at manipulating people. People had to be generous to start with, but then I had to get them to believe a story so they would give me money.

I hitchhiked for two reasons. First, I hitchhiked to get from

one place to another. But that probably wasn't the most important reason because most of the time I didn't really have a place to go. I was this stray dog going back and forth. But the second reason was always important. That was to talk people out of money. You are in the car with someone for several hours, and you have a chance to get under their skin.

I found that 50% to 75% of the people gave me money when they let me out. It ranged from a few dollars to as much as $100. I was very good at manipulating people. I could get money out of them in a way that they thought it was their idea, and they were happy to do it. I would get people to buy me meals. I would take out a can of cold soup and tell them that's what I was going to eat. I knew the impact that would have on them. They usually offered to buy me supper.

One time we were coming out of Dallas in the middle of the winter. I think I was coming home for Christmas. The driver asked me if I had anything to eat, and I said, NO. He took me to this truck stop. I was going to order a burger, and he said, "No, no. no. You eat whatever. I'm buying. I'm buying." So, I had a big old hamburger steak. When we were finished he reached in his pocket to pay the check and pulled out of a roll of bills. He paid the bill, and then he peeled off a twenty and said, "Here, you take this." Then he pulled out another twenty, "Here, you take this one." Then he handed me a ten and then handed me another twenty.

There was another guy who picked me up in Iowa. He was driving to Mankato. But he drove me all the way up to the Twin Cities and bought me a hotel room. He went way out of his way. He was an insurance salesman, and he was a Christian. I knew something about the Bible, and I could "talk the Bible" with him.

He was just a kind man. I think he believed that I needed Jesus Christ, and he wanted to help me. He wanted to show me what Christ was about—the goodness and the kindness.

Sometimes people asked me what I was doing. I found that a lot of people wished that they could do what I was doing—that they had the courage to leave everything and do what I was doing.

There were many people who said, "Oh, I wish I dared do what you are doing." They didn't have the guts to do it. They didn't dare be without money. There were a lot of times that I woke up with a dime in my pocket. That was it. I didn't even have a cigarette. They were frozen by fear—the fear of not having anything. They were impressed with my courage.

Of course the real story was that this was the only thing I knew. I had quit everything else. It was the only thing I knew—bum around the country and beg from people, get people to be good to me, take advantage of good people.

You have all kinds of experiences when you are hitchhiking. I've had rides from 5 miles to 1500 miles. I had one fellow driving a semi, pick me up outside San Diego and drive straight through to Dallas—about 1500 miles. He bought the meals and gave me $20 bucks when I left him in Dallas. We were in the cab of his truck, smoking weed and doing amphetamines. This was in the late 1970's. We drove straight through. He was strung out on speed. We stopped every now and then to get coffee and a bite to eat. We talked and talked, and he fed me "Black Beauties" (amphetamines). Speed made your hair tingle, and you got jittery. You would talk a lot, and it kept you awake. You had so many kinds of speed in those days —Black Beauties, Pink Hearts and Cross Tops.

It was possible to hitchike for days without anybody saying a nice thing to you. Sometimes they would grumble and growl at you. Sometimes a person would pick you up and start rambling about how hitchhikers were the scum of the earth. I've left vehicles when the abuse got too bad. I was in Utah one time, coming out of Salt Lake, and this Mormon man picked me up on my way back to San Diego. He was a solid, hard core Mormon and driving a pickup truck. He started in. "What are you doing with your life?"

"Well, I'm not sure right now."

"Well, my son, he's about your age and he's out on a mission. He's a missionary. Why aren't you doing something like that?"

He kept on, telling me I was doing nothing with my life and how worthless I was. Finally I said, "Let me out. Just let me out." The next stop sign he let me out. I couldn't take it anymore. He was going a long ways too.

Another time I was outside Houston, Texas. I am standing there hitchhiking with a buddy of mine. We're hitchhiking together, and this guy pulled over. We asked, "How far are you going?"

"As far as you want to go."

That sounded pretty good. There was already somebody in the front passenger seat, so we got in the back seat, and he took off. He was doing about 100 miles an hour weaving in and out of traffic.

I said, "This is as far as I wanna go. Let me out."

He stopped, and all three of us got out.

Sometimes my ride would be going a long ways, and when it grew dark, he looked for a place to stop for the night. One time I had my bedroll in my backpack and the driver stopped in Mile City, Montana. He said, "I'm going to find me a hotel." Then he asked me where I was going to sleep. I said, "I'll probably be sleeping under the bridge over there. Will you stop and pick me up again tomorrow morning please?"

He said, "Naw, it's cold outside. Come with me. You can sleep on my floor."

I did stay for a little while with a couple outside Detroit Lakes, Minnesota. They had a giant chicken farm. I stayed with them and helped them build some buildings. What I liked was I could wake up in the morning, open up the fridge and grab a beer. They were recent German immigrants. I slept in their bunkhouse. I was the only one in the bunkhouse, but they had about 13 kids.

I stayed with them for a week, ten days. They were supposed to have a half million chickens. One night I went to town and got drunk with several of their boys. The next morning I woke up about 6 o'clock in the bunkhouse. I was thirsty and hot. The beers were all gone, and I didn't have any water. That's when I saw these six muskmelons in the guy's garden. Those muskmelons looked juicy. I ate all six of this guy's melons. I couldn't stop. He was furious when he came out and saw what was left of the rinds. They were beautiful muskmelons.

### Books, but not signs

When I was hitchhiking I never used a sign. It never seemed to do any good. I just stood there with my thumb out. Sometimes I would sit on my backpack and read a book. I was reading a lot in those days—all kinds of books. Mostly I read psychological thrillers, but I read everything. If I didn't have anything else, I'd pick up a romance novel—something to occupy my mind. I'd sit on my backpack, read a book and wait for someone to pull over.

I learned some things about hitchhiking. First, you want to be where there is a lot of traffic. Second, in a lot of places you've got to stand at the top of the ramp because there is no hitchhiking on the Interstate. So, you want to get near a truck stop where there's a lot of traffic, standing at the top of the ramp. It varied from state to state where you could hitch hike. I never got arrested for hitch hiking but I've been told to get off the freeway.

### Stuck

Sometimes I found myself stuck in the middle of nowhere. That's probably the worst part of hitchhiking. I've been dropped off in places where there was nothing. One time a guy picked me up in

Kansas and asked me where I was going. I said "Minneapolis."

He said, "Me too."

He dropped me off in Minneapolis, Kansas. The town was off the freeway in the middle of nowhere. There wasn't a whole lot in western Kansas - not a whole lot of traffic, not a whole lot of anything. I stood there for about eight hours, and finally somebody picked me up.

**Toyah, Texas was deserted.**

It was even worse in Toyah, Texas. I got dropped off in Toyah, and there was nothing but a gas station and restaurant combined—one building. That was all. I stood at that ramp for hours and hours and hours. I was at the top of the freeway entrance ramp for I-20.

There was very little traffic of any kind. It was a hottest part of the summer, and many drivers preferred to take I-40 which is farther north to avoid some of the heat. I stood there for eight hours in the broiling sun. No one stopped. I had nothing to eat or drink. That night I slept under the bridge, and in the morning I returned to that same spot at the top of the ramp.

This old cowboy drove by in his pickup truck. He rolled down the window and shouted, "I ain't going anywhere but here's a few beers to keep you going." He handed me four cans of beer. Then he drove across the median and headed in the opposite direction. I was terribly thirsty. I hadn't had anything to eat or drink. I didn't have any money in my pocket. I couldn't even go over to the restaurant and buy a cup of coffee or anything. I was so grateful for those four beers.

I stood there and I stood there and I stood there. Four hours later he came by again. "You still here?" He handed me four more beers. Again he drove across the median and headed in the other direction. He did this four times. I was there at least a day and a half before I finally got a ride. My only saving grace was that old cowboy.

### I almost hit bottom

You start getting really frustrated and really depressed when you wonder if you will ever get a ride. The first time I ever thought about killing myself was the time I was hitchhiking out of San Diego. I was heading east from San Diego, and I got as far as the outskirts of Phoenix, Arizona. I was sitting under a bridge. I had spent my last five dollars getting a 12-pack and a bag of Doritos. I lived on Doritos and 12-packs for a long time. I was sitting under the bridge drinking the 12-pack, eating those Doritos and watching the trucks go by at 80 miles an hour. I had just turned 19. For the previous year I had been on the streets of San Diego, eating out of dumpsters. I didn't feel like I belonged anywhere. I didn't feel like anybody gave a shit. I was sitting under this bridge watching trucks flying by at 80 miles an hour. I was thinking how easy it'd be to step out in front of one of them. I really contemplated doing that. I finished that 12-pack and got down on the freeway, not sure what I was going to do. Right away two guys from Minnesota picked me up. They were going about 80 miles an hour too, but when they saw me, they pulled over and stopped for me. They were from Long Prairie, Minnesota, and they were heading to Kansas.

They had beer. They had smokes. They had weed. They gave me a ride up into Kansas. They may have saved my life at that time. I never told them how close I came to killing myself. I just told them how grateful I was. I told them I was really depressed and needed to get back to Minnesota. I explained I might still have a home in Minnesota. I really need to get there.

They didn't have any money—just gas money. But they let me drink their beer and smoke their pot. They said they understood not having anything. I don't know if they had ever been in my shoes or not. But they seemed to understand. They might have saved my life. Another 24 hours under that bridge and I might have taken my life.

Looking back I can see that the 1970's and 1980's were the golden age of hitchhiking. In those days getting from Kansas City to Minneapolis was no problem. People picked up hitch hikers back then. One time I made it from Rochester, Minnesota, to Dallas, Texas, in one day—one 24-hour day—hitchhiking.

### A LOT OF WOMEN PICKED ME UP

I suppose I wasn't dressed very well when I was hitchhiking, but if someone was going to pick me up—my dress wasn't a deterrent. That was my experience. I had a lot of women pick me up. They said I looked "safe."

Sometimes a woman made a pass at me. One gal took me home with her to Missouri. I stayed with her for a few days. But she had five kids. I hung around with her for a while, but I couldn't take all the screaming children. This was when I was about 20, before I had kids of my own. I think all five of these kids had different dads. She lived out in the country, outside a small town. When she took me home, at first I was wondering, "What is this woman doing? Is she taking me out to the woods to kill me or what?"

Hitchhiking was lonely—very lonely. I lost who I was in that period of time. Once in a while you ran into another hitchhiker that you could talk to and party with for a little bit. Then you went your separate ways. You might spend a day or two under a bridge together, but it was very difficult to hitchhike with two people.

Recently hitchhiking has become more dangerous. Ninety-five percent of the hitchhikers are just trying to get from one place to another, but you got that five percent that ruined it for everybody. It's just like riding a freight train. The reason the train people get so mad at you is that a small minority of freight train riders have broken into containers. That's why the railroad security men would throw you in jail if they caught you.

### My first freight train ride - love at first sight

I had recently turned 20. It was late summer of 1979, and I was in Billings, Montana where I had a girlfriend. I was bouncing back and forth from Billings to Minneapolis and back to Billings. I found out that my brother Bob was getting married. My brother Bruce was in Denver. That's all I knew. He was homeless too. So, I decided that I would go down to Denver and make sure that Bruce knew about Bob getting married.

This guy in Billings asked, "Can I go with you?"

I said "Sure." So we headed out hitchhiking together.

We made it to about 30 miles outside of Denver, and this guy asked me, "Where does your brother live?"

"I don't know."

"Well, where does your brother work?"

"I don't know."

"So, how are you going to find your brother?"

"I don't know."

We got into Denver, and we slept under a bridge near the railroad tracks that night. The next morning, we got up and walked to the Capitol Hill Park in Denver. I was sitting in the park asking myself, "If I were Bruce here in Denver, where would I be?" At that moment, Bruce appeared walking toward the park. I hadn't been in Denver but 12 hours, and there he was. I suppose Bruce and I thought alike. I learned that the night before he had been camped out two bridges down from me. He had been there for a month. He was homeless at the time—working out of a "slave market" for day laborers.

I told Bruce about the wedding, and we agreed we would

both go back to McIntosh together. Bruce suggested we ride a freight train. I thought, "Cool. I had never ridden a freight train." So, we worked all week out of the slave market and earned some money. Then we bought a couple cases of beer, a jug of whiskey, some LSD and some pot.

We got on that train, and I fell in love with the train. It was my first freight train ride. I loved the ride—the rocking back and forth, the freedom that I felt. We were in a boxcar. There was a sense of freedom—that nobody could touch you. You were out in the elements. You were actually going someplace. You didn't have to sit and wait and wait and wait for a ride. Once you got on, you knew you were going for 500 miles.

In the early days I rode box cars but later I rode twin stacks—the flat cars with two containers stacked one on top the other. There is a little opening at the end of the flat car—just big enough for one guy to lie down. Those are really smooth rides. A lot of times there are electronics and other expensive and fragile stuff in these containers, so the railroad cars are designed to run smooth.

But in the early days it was boxcars. We left the door open. We would spike the door. We would take a railroad spike and cram it into the door jamb so the door wouldn't slide shut. I learned to look into the boxcar to make sure it was empty. If someone was already in the car, you didn't get in unless they invited you. It was the rules of the road.

I didn't like riding with other people because you didn't know who you were getting involved with. Riding a freight train was more dangerous than hitch hiking. The people riding freight trains were sometimes crazy people. By the time you were riding freight trains, you were so far out of society. You had worked your way into your own little fringe society—the freight train society.

Before you got on the train you had to come with everything you needed. You made sure you had a little bit of food, some tobacco, a gallon of water. You peed right out the door, and you crapped into a shopping bag, and you flung that out the door. But a train would usually stop every few hours. You knew you were going to stop at least every eight hours for a crew change. So you were able to get off that train at that time.

You learned what to carry and what not to carry on a train. For example, you didn't carry bread because you would end up with smashed bread. So you carried tortillas. They're flat already. Here is another trick. Let's say you wanted a cup of hot coffee and a bowl of hot ramen noodles. You would take two beer cans full of water and a fusie. A fusie is a road flare. You light that road flare and stick it next to the beer cans. You keep moving it around those beer cans. The fusies would last five or ten minutes. When that fuse was gone, you would have two boiling cans of water. So you could make your ramen noodles and your coffee. You could do all this while the train was doing 50 miles an hour. You could use anything dehydrated. It was nice to get dehydrated food when you could because it was light and easy to prepare. When you got on a train, you should have a gallon of water.

### Never be without your "credit card" – a magic marker

I learned the most important things to bring aboard a freight train. I would say that number one on the list was clean socks. You wanted as many pairs of extra socks as possible. You were on your feet so much; you wanted to take care of your feet. You wanted fresh, clean socks. Number two was booze. You wanted a case of beer plus a jug of whiskey or vodka. Number three was a good bedroll—a good sleeping bag. I've had bed rolls that were almost five feet around because they included a five-inch pad underneath. The pad kept me off the ground in the winter time. Weed wasn't that important as long as I had alcohol. A jug of water was right up at the top. You could go anywhere if you had a jug of water and a bedroll. Next, you needed a magic marker. A magic marker was very important. You could make a sign. "Homeless. Need money." It was like a credit card. Wherever you went, you could find a piece of cardboard to make a sign, but you had to bring your own magic marker. A magic marker was my credit card.

### DELIVERING THE U.S. MAIL

In the spring of 1979 my brother-in-law, Paul Aakhus, was looking for some extra income. Paul was the husband of my sister, Bev. He was trying to make extra money to supplement his struggling dairy farm, so he subcontracted a U.S. Mail route. Then he hired me to run it.

I had a one-ton Chevy truck that I drove. I picked up mail in nine little towns and dropped it off at the distribution center in Detroit Lakes, Minnesota. I drove along US Highway 2 and Route 59 to all these little towns. I would unload and then load back up. I would drive over to Brainerd. I would sit there for a couple of hours and load back up, drive back to Detroit Lakes and sit there for a little bit and then drive home again. Every night I drove 400 miles, and Paul paid me $200 a week cash—which was pretty good money in '79. I went to work at five in the afternoon and got done at seven in the morning. But I had a lot of layover time in there. Sometimes I would take a nap when I had a three-hour layover in Detroit Lakes. It was all night-time driving. Maybe this was the break I needed. I had steady work. I was settling down. I was back in Minnesota. I was around my family.

The U.S. Postal Service required an application and background check, and I filled this out in April when I started. Then in November they sent me a letter saying "Because of your arrest

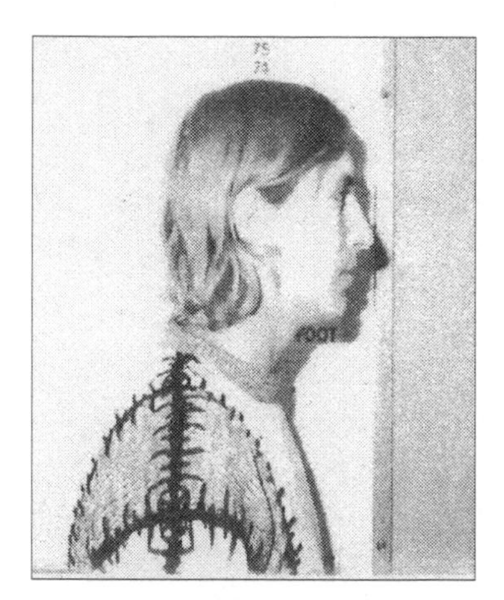

**I was 20 year old for this 1979 mug shot.**

record (for breaking and entering Sylvia's 3.2 bar when I was 16), we feel that the security of the mail is endangered. Therefore you are terminated immediately."

So I was fired from delivering the U.S. Mail. Now the people I worked with at all these little post offices encouraged me to stick around. They said, "We'll get you back on the route." But in my infinite wisdom I took off for the West Coast. It was right around Thanksgiving in 1979. A month later I hitchhiked back to Minnesota.

Now it was getting toward Christmas time. I went up to International Falls to visit Uncle Dean, my mom's brother. Uncle Dean operated a small business cleaning banks, and he had a nervous breakdown. So I went up to take care of his business. He cleaned four banks and a couple other businesses. This job represented another opportunity for me to settle down.

One night after I finished my work, I went to a bar. I drank a quart of whiskey in about 45 minutes. I remembered going to the bar, but that's the last thing I remembered. The guy that was with me at the bar wouldn't ride with me. He lived about four miles outside of town, and he said, "I'll walk home." He told me about this the next day. I don't remember leaving the bar, but the next thing I knew there was a cop knocking on my car window. The car was still in gear, motor was running, and I was in a ditch in front of the house of the mayor of International Falls.

I went to jail. My blood alcohol level was .42. As soon as they found out how high it was, they took me to detox in Virginia, Minnesota.

That was my first DWI. The typical sentence was a $300 fine or 30 days in jail. Mom went to court with me and was willing to give them $300. But the judge was really mad at me because my blood alcohol was so high. He increased the fine to $500. So, Mom said, "I ain't got it." I told my mom not to worry about it. I told her I didn't want her money anyway. I spent 30 days in jail.

### "Two girls and they're both pretty hot"

I got out of jail in January of 1980, and that spring I found work seeding grain in Hillsborough, North Dakota. I earned about $1500 that spring. I was drinking steadily but I managed to work. I was working with my buddy, Mike Bjerken. It was early May. We were staying with Mike's mom at her house. Mike said, "Some people are returning from Oregon. They used to live here. There are two girls, and they're both pretty hot."

So, we were working in his mom's garden when this car pulled up. The family got out including these two girls. I pointed at one and told Mike, "She's mine. I'm going to take her to bed." The one that interested me was Betty, and her sister was Mary. I didn't take Betty to bed, but we dated a few times. I liked Betty right away. She was attractive. She seemed like a normal girl.

But soon I was off on another escapade. I was in Billings, Montana. I ran out of money, so I found a day's work at the Salvation Army in town—picking up donated clothes and furniture. They paid me $100 cash. I was walking down the street, and this guy drove by and shouted to me, "Hey, you wanna go drink with a couple girls?" I didn't know this guy from Adam. He said, "There's two girls. You wanna go drink with me with them?"

I thought, "Yeah. Why not?"

Well, I slept with Mary the first night and moved in with the Roxy the next day. I dated Roxy off and on for six months. I would hitch hike back to Minneapolis and get some drugs hitch hike back to Billings.

While I was going back and forth between Montana and Minnesota, Betty was back in Minnesota dating a buddy of mine. On my way back in the spring of 1980 I got my second DWI. I wound up in jail in Elk River, Minnesota. They sent me to treatment in Fergus Falls. I got out of treatment and went up to East Grand Forks to a halfway house. I stayed there for a couple of weeks.

Then I went back to McIntosh. I found that Betty and her sister Mary were still there. Betty and I started hanging out together. What I especially liked was that she drank with me on the back of the lion. We had this park called Lion's Park that had a statue of a big lion. We would climb up on the back of that lion and drink. When she did that with me, I thought, "This is my kind of girl." One thing led to another, and I believe it was June of '81 that we slept together for the first time.

### "I'm pregnant"

After a couple months I began hiding from Betty. I didn't want to be with her any more. She was aware that I was withdrawing from her, and she stalked me. She chased me down. I was in Hillsborough, North Dakota, at the time. I was working on a large farm, sitting on a tractor, working 12-hour days. She came to be with me in Hillsborough. It was the end of August, we were together, and suddenly she said, "I'm pregnant." Just like that. I suspected it anyway, but she just threw it at me.

I didn't know what to do. I wanted to be there for her because I had already gone through one abortion. I was scared that that was going to happen again. But I was drinking, and I was

**Betty**

terrified. She was a pretty girl. She had a car. She had money. I was living in the park in McIntosh off and on. She would pick me up in her car and drive me around. I would drink her booze and spend her money. I was perfectly content to do that. But then she got pregnant and I thought, "God, I don't want to be with this woman." I felt that she would tie me down, and I would lose my freedom. She was pretty possessive, and I think she was mentally ill.

So, I left. I didn't say anything to Betty. I had a car at the time, and I took off and ended up in the state of Washington picking apples. I wasn't making much money. Then my car broke down. So, I hitch hiked down to Texas. Now Christmas was approaching. I remember sitting on a stone ledge in downtown Dallas. It was right before Christmas. I was thinking, "Oh, God, what am I doing? I've got another child out there."

# 4

# Married, with Children

## "We're getting married"

I was sitting on a stone bench in Dallas, Texas, and I did some hard thinking. Betty was now about six or seven months pregnant. I hadn't said a word to her since I took off. She had no idea where I was or what the future was for her and her kid. Finally, I decided. "I better go home and take care of this kid." So, I went back to Minnesota and I told Betty we were getting married. I didn't ask her. I said, "We're getting married."

She was seven months pregnant. We got married on January 6, 1982, at the parsonage of the Mt. Carmel Church in McIntosh. It was an American Free Lutheran church. The pastor married us in his home. My brother Bruce stood up for me, and her mom stood up for her. I was 22, and Betty was 18. This was only my third real relationship. I had Janet, then a girl out in California, and now

**Betty and John about the time of their wedding in January 1982**

**John, the pastor holding newborn Jeremy and Betty at the time of his baptism in early 1982**

Betty. I liked Betty, but I don't know if I loved her. There were no photographs. There was no big celebration. I married her because she was pregnant.

My dad had a struggling dairy farm in McIntosh, and he persuaded me to move to the farm and help him with the operation. My dad had a few cows at the time. Four hours after I got married, I was back at the farm milking cows. That was my honeymoon. My mom reminded me, "You already had your honeymoon."

A couple days after the wedding at the parsonage, we had a reception. This was at my brother Bill's house. It was the biggest house in our family. It was the house I grew up in. Bill bought that house. A few people showed up—mostly family. I drank away almost all my old friends. For wedding gifts we got a lot of stuff for the baby. That's what we needed.

Mom had moved back in with Dad when I was 16, and she stayed with him until I was 23. So at the time of our wedding, they were living together on his dairy farm. The farm had a compound of small buildings. Mom and Dad were living in a shack that he had built for them. He offered me and Betty a trailer house to live in. That living arrangement lasted only about six weeks. I got into a big fight with Dad, and we left.

In early March we moved to Crookston. Betty was nine months pregnant. Jeremy was born March 15, 1982. I was in the delivery room. I was so excited to see this little boy being born. The doctor handed him to me right away, and I held him. He was a big nine-pound baby boy. Tears came to my eyes. It just drew me into being a Dad.

I was scared to death. I didn't know what to do. I was so excited and scared. We brought him home. When we first brought Jeremy home, he was in a little bassinet for about three weeks in our bedroom. Then I set up the crib in our bedroom because he was getting too big. After Jeremy was born, something changed inside me. I thought maybe this was it. Maybe this will settle me down. I finally got my boy. I was so proud to be a father.

Betty tried breast feeding Jeremy for a little bit but she wound up in the hospital with a staph infection. So we switched to the bottle. That meant I could feed him. I was very involved. I did a lot of feeding in the middle of the night. I changed his diapers. I bathed him in the kitchen sink. I bathed him there for a long time—until he got old enough to sit up. Then we moved to the bathtub. I had this beautiful little boy that was mine. This was my boy. Betty knew that Jeremy was my boy. She thought he was a miniature version of me.

I showed Jeremy off to family and friends. To anyone that would listen, I said, "Look, this is my boy." I called him "Sunshine" because he was the sunshine of my life.

### I was good for six – eight months

I finally felt like I belonged somewhere. Maybe this was it. Maybe this event would change everything. Maybe I would get sober. I felt good being a dad. Maybe I would get a decent job and become a decent husband. I was good for six–eight months. I was on the wagon. I really, really wanted to make things work. It was very, very hard to stop drinking. I was smoking weed at the time but I wasn't drinking. On a rare occasion, for example, when I went to a concert in Fargo, I went on a big drunk. But then I'd go home, and I would stay sober. I couldn't figure out what triggered me to start drinking. I guess I just wanted to drink more than I wanted to stay sober.

**John is proudly showing off "Sunshine" to his father in 1982**

Within a year I started drinking off and on. A lot of times I was stressed out about something. I didn't really have a good idea of what a family was supposed to be. I didn't have any role models of how to be a good husband or to be a real dad. I had been shown everything that was wrong. Most of the time I was a very good father. I had Jeremy with me a lot. He was a happy little boy. I was happy too.

Then my dad talked me into moving back to McIntosh, back to his place again to try to make a go of the dairy farm. I was there off and on, off and on for about 18 months from the fall of 1982 until the spring of 1984. I would take off and go on drunks. I would disappear for a week or two at a time. There was a young fellow living on the compound, and he would have to milk the cows and take care of things whenever I was gone.

I had some really happy times with Betty. One time when Jeremy was about three months old, Betty and I went to Fargo to visit Betty's sister. Her sister lived in a tiny apartment. We were all partying, having a good time. We had Jeremy sleeping in the bathtub, and I remember I felt so close to Betty at that time. We were enjoying each other. We were newly married. I was learning to love this woman. After we got married I thought to myself, "She's the mother of my children."

Another time a bunch of us went to the drive-in theater in Bemidji. Jeremy was only about four months old. It was Betty and I, and Betty's sister, Mary, and her friend Mike. We stuck Jeremy in the back window where he fell fast asleep. So, Betty and I had special times like this. We learned to love each other.

### Jeremy's first steps

Jeremy started crawling out of his crib when he was 10 months old. He climbed right out of his crib. I think I pushed Jeremy really, really hard. I wanted him to walk. I wanted him to talk. He started really young at things.

Jeremy was talking really plain by the time he was 15 months. He called water "watier." A quarter would be a "quartier." "A dollier" for a dollar. I loved to listen to him.

I remember Jeremy's first steps. Jeremy had been crawling and then walking along by holding unto the furniture. He had been doing this for a while. One day when Betty and I were sitting there on the floor, he let go and walked right over to me. Then he realized what he had done, and he fell down.

The first thing Jeremy said was "Dah." He was talking to me. I used to give Betty a hard time about that. He said my name first. I would make him laugh by blowing on his belly. I would play peek-a-boo with him. I loved his silly antics. We had a big dog – part St. Bernard, part Husky, part German Shepherd. This dog was vicious toward adults, but Jeremy could climb on him and pull his ears, and this dog would take it. It was funny looking at the dog's expression. It seemed to say, "Awwww. Get this kid off me."

### Josh is born

Jeremy made me feel like I belonged. Now I really, really had something. Betty and I were getting along pretty good. We talked about having another boy. For some reason I knew it would be a boy. When I was younger, I pictured myself having two sons. Soon I got my second son. All we had to do was talk about it, and Betty got pregnant. She got pregnant real easy. Josh was born November 23, 1983. By the time Josh was born I was more settled down. I didn't push him as hard.

From the beginning Josh was quiet and laid back. Josh and Jeremy were opposites. Jeremy was always active—always getting into things. Not Josh. He was easy going, quiet and patient. When he was little he always put his finger in his belly button. When he grew older, he could sit and play by himself for hours. He was soon playing with Legos. He loved them.

**Josh (right) is putting his finger in his belly button while Jeremy tries to imitate him.**

I really, really wanted to make this work. When Josh was born I felt complete. I had these two beautiful boys. I had a beautiful wife. We were getting along pretty good. We didn't fight. We didn't argue. But… my drinking got in the way.

For 18 months I kept trying to get the dairy farm in McIntosh going. Of course I was still drinking all the time. Betty worked a lot of evenings. She was working at the nursing home when Josh was born. Three weeks after he was born, she was back to work. She worked evenings, and I got both the boys.

I had a little work, but Betty relied on welfare. I was never stable enough to support my family. We would get off welfare for a little bit. Then I would go off on a drunk, and Betty would get back on welfare. This happened repeatedly. I was never on welfare myself, but of course I lived there with them. I would get a job and would think that maybe this would last, and she would go off welfare. I would work some place four or five months and then I'd go off on a drunk.

Really early it was clear that Jeremy was more like me, and Josh was more like Betty. It started with Betty telling me how much Jeremy looked like me and acted like me. Just before Josh was born, Betty told me that she saw the devil in Jeremy. She kind of pushed him away after that. Then she always said he was just like me. Maybe she saw the devil in me.

One time Bruce and I were building a horse barn. Bruce smashed his finger with a hammer. There were just the three of us there—Bruce and I and Jeremy. When Bruce hit his thumb with that hammer Bruce and I just looked at each other, neither of us said anything, but Jeremy said, "Oh shit." It was just so appropriate. He was about two years old. It was so appropriate we both burst out laughing.

Jeremy entertained his uncle Bruce a lot. I was so tickled. My little boy was out there with his uncle. It was so fulfilling to watch my son bring pleasure to members of my family.

Because Jeremy was my first child, he changed my life when he was born. And when Josh came along, I felt completed. They both sat in my lap. They both hugged and kissed. We were very, very close. I was very affectionate with them. My mom taught me that. I told the boys I loved them. I hugged them and held them and kissed them goodnight.

### Good times

When the boys were little, we had this really big yard with a garage, a shed, and a nice garden. I worked in the garden. It was one of my special pleasures. Before I would go to work in the morning, I would go out there and pick a few weeds. Every evening when I got home, I would check out my garden. I had beans and peas, corn, radishes and carrots—all the normal stuff you grow in a garden. Here and there, scattered throughout the garden, I planted a flower such as a geranium to add some color.

My mom came over one day. When she saw those flowers in my garden, she started crying. I said, "What's wrong, Mom?" She said, "Your grandfather used to do that." He introduced patches of beauty into his garden. I never knew that.

I haven't had a garden since the boys were little. I enjoyed gardening. I enjoyed working in the soil. I enjoyed watching things grow, picking my own vegetables. The boys would go out and pull up carrots and eat them right out of the ground. A little bit of dirt always makes the carrot taste better.

There were times when Betty and I would sit and play "Scrabble" in the evening when she wasn't working. I enjoyed spending that quality time with Betty—having fun, doing something we both enjoyed. We would make homemade ice cream with the old fashioned hand crank. We'd do sleigh rides in the winter time and hay rides in the summer. It was Betty and I, Jeremy and Josh. Our family had two sleighs. My dad had the larger sleigh. I had the smaller sleigh.

I would bring the boys into the bathtub with me, and we played soap hockey. You flip the soap so it whips around the tub. We made games out of everything. I loved these little boys so much. It was like they completed me.

I talked to my boys all the time. I talked with them like they were adults. I never baby-talked to them. That kept them from baby talking. I would tell them stories. I would read a book, but then I would make up the story as we turned the page. Just about every night I read them a bedtime story. I started reading to them when they were a year old. I read to them until they were six and eight. They were interested in these crazy stories that Dad would come up with. Usually we had a little snack of fruit or something while I read. I would finish reading to them and then they would fall asleep.

I was in town having coffee one night, and Jeremy got burned in the kitchen—a pot of boiling carrots spilled on him. Betty had to call the restaurant to have me come home because Jeremy kept crying, "I want my Dad." As soon as I got home, he settled down. I have to admit that I was very proud that he called for me.

Betty and I almost never gave each other presents. We both had the opinion that we would be decent to each other all the time, rather than do something special one day. We tried to do little things for each other. I would stop in the middle of the road and pick a handful of wildflowers to bring home to her. She was always very appreciative that I took the time to think of her.

We had some romantic times. We took weekends off, just the two us. My mom took the boys. We would have dinner at a favorite place, then stay at a nice hotel. Betty would drive because I didn't have a driver's license. We would take the time for each other—to slow down and appreciate each other. We didn't talk about our relationship a lot. We didn't talk about important things a lot. I suppose our communication was not real good.

Betty took really good care of my children. That was important to me. She made sure they were clean and fed. She knew that that they were the most important thing to me – those two boys. I spent hours playing catch with them in our backyard. Baseball was my favorite sport.

Betty was a very good looking woman. She carried on a conversation with me. She was intelligent. She wasn't real well educated. She was a high school drop out. But she had a lot of intelligence. Most of the time she was very pleasant to be around.

### But we had problems lurking beneath the surface

But there were always problems lurking. Betty seldom smiled. She was never really at peace with herself. She had mental illness. Her dad had moved the family back and forth, back and forth from Oregon to Minnesota every year or so. She never really settled into one place. She never had friends.

She was moody and unpredictable. For example, she would invite people over, and then she would go hide in her room. When they arrived, I had to entertain them. Or sometimes she would walk into the bedroom in a really good mood and come out crabby five minutes later. It was really, really hard to deal with. Sometimes she was suicidal. She didn't really talk to me about it, but I believe she heard voices. These terrible mood swings would drive me away.

One winter day I took the kids with me a couple of miles out of Erskine. There was a giant hill on the golf course. I took the kids out there sledding on a plastic sheet. Betty was supposed to meet us, but she didn't come. So I took the boys, and we started walking down U.S. Highway 2. There wasn't a whole lot of traffic. I got the kids on the inside away from the traffic. Betty finally arrived and shouted, "What the hell are you doing with my kids here in the middle of the highway?"

"Betty, these are my kids too, and they're not in the middle of the highway. They are safe." She just blew up. That sent her into the mental health unit. I drove her over there, and she went in voluntarily. She was in and out of the mental health unit the whole marriage.

Of course, I had my own problems. I had at least two obsessions then. I had an obsession to drink, and I also had an obsession to run. Her unpredictable moods fed my obsession to drink, because I knew that once I had a few drinks, I would feel alright.

It was at that time, that I realized that I was depressed too. I was dealing with my own mental illness. So, I self-medicated—with alcohol. At home Betty hated my drinking. She knew that drinking would land me in jail for DWI's. Betty drank a lot when we were dating, but she quit as soon as she got pregnant. She saw alcohol as the curse of her marriage, and my drinking was getting worse.

Several times Betty and I drove down to the Cities with the boys. Sometimes we went to Minneapolis to see the Twins play. That was a big adventure to drive all the way down to Minneapolis for a baseball game at the Metrodome. We stayed in town for a day or two. We walked around downtown Minneapolis, and we looked at all the big buildings. We stayed in a hotel out in Eagan that we heard wasn't too expensive. We did this several times with the boys.

On one of those trips we took the boys to the big zoo south of downtown Minneapolis. Josh was about two – just in the process of being potty trained. We lived out in the country, so whenever he wasn't inside the house he could whip it out to pee almost any place. Now we were in the food court at the Minnesota Zoo, and we were eating lunch. All of a sudden Josh whipped out his wiener and started peeing right in the food court. He didn't wet his pants. He was doing what he had learned. What could I say? Everybody was laughing. I was a little bit embarrassed.

In Erskine, everybody knew we had a team of horses and did sleigh rides. So, when Senator Roger Moe planned a 14th birthday party for his daughter, he asked us to provide a sleigh ride for the

**John driving the horse and sleigh with Betty and the boys**

party. When we provided the sleigh ride for Roger Moe and his kids, Betty was really proud of me. I felt good. Betty felt good. Roger Moe was the Speaker of the House here in Minnesota. I knew Roger Moe. I had been up to his office in the Capitol building. I later learned that he posted a photograph of that sleigh ride on the wall of his office at the Capitol building. It meant that much to him. It probably meant even more to me. Betty was proud of me.

**A Christmas photo with Betty holding Josh and John holding Jeremy**

One year we sealed off the upstairs, and we gave the boys the first floor bedroom, and Betty and I moved down to the basement bedroom. One morning I heard these little feet pitter pattering down the steps. Into our bed they came—these two little tow heads. It just melted my heart. Gradually our fridge was covered with their drawings—stick people they had drawn and colored pictures from their coloring books. They were usually signed, "Love, Josh" or "Love, Jeremy." As they got older they wrote notes on them usually ending, "Love you, Dad."

I made a lot of homemade cookies. I baked homemade donuts. Nothing came out of a box. I made everything from scratch. I made birthday cakes from scratch.

My oldest niece Michelle, and my youngest boy, Josh, had the same birthday. They were seven years apart. The year that Josh turned three, he was really into Sesame Street. Sesame Street was featuring a two-headed monster at the time. So I made a two-headed monster birthday cake for Joshua and my niece Michelle. The birthday party was held up at my sister's place. We did a lot of family gatherings at my sister's. Everybody loved that two-headed monster birthday cake. I took the time to do things like that for my boys. They were so important to me. I tried to make special things for them—whenever I could.

### My disappearing acts

I think it was in 1986 that I suddenly received $800 from the federal government. It was a grant to give me money to buy a chain saw to cut my own firewood. I had access to a forest where I could harvest firewood. Now I had this $800 in my pocket. I was going down to buy a chain saw when I met my buddy Larry Braulick. Larry said he was going to take off for Texas. I joined Larry and another friend, Buff, and we wound up drinking in Halstead, Minnesota. We drank until the bar closed up. Then we drove to Fargo to continued our drinking. Buff drove his pickup.

Fargo led to Sioux Falls and first thing you know, we were in Oklahoma and then Texas.

We let Larry off in Tyler, Texas, which was his destination. He wouldn't let Buff and me come into the house because we were too drunk. So, we got mad at him and decided we were going to California. We stopped at the Seven Eleven in El Paso to fill the pickup with gas and add a quart of oil. Suddenly there were about ten cop cars surrounding us. There had been a rash of burglaries at the Seven Eleven. The police were on the look out for suspects. I supposed we looked suspicious. We were drunker than skunks. The cop said, "Who's driving?"

Although I had been driving, I didn't have a license, so Buff said, "I am."

"Well, we need to search your car."

Suddenly the keys fell out of my jacket pocket. So the cops knew that I had been driving. In searching the vehicle, they found all sorts of beer.

"What are you guys doing?"

"Oh, we're on vacation."

The cop looked at us, "There's the freeway. New Mexico is 12 miles that way. Go."

We woke up the next morning in Arizona. We had slept in the pickup. We had been sleeping in the pickup the whole time. My $800 had been reduced to $20 bucks, and Buff had $25. We decided maybe we had enough money to get home.

So we took off for Minnesota. We hit a snowstorm in New Mexico. The only things running were semi's and our pickup. This lasted until we got into South Dakota. Wc were out of money, so Buff finally took out his checkbook and wrote a check in South Dakota for enough cash to get us back to Minnesota. He had money in the bank. It was quite an adventure. I was gone for 11,12 days.

When I walked in the door, Betty said, "Where the hell have you been?"

I said, "I wound up in Arizona."

"No you didn't. You've been screwing around again."

### Drinkin', cheatin' and disappearin'

I had given Betty reason to think the worst of me. I carried on an affair with a neighbor woman in Erskine, and a couple gals in Crookston. I didn't really feel bad about cheating. I didn't have much of a conscience back then. Betty had to have been aware of it. The neighbor lived two houses over. Her husband and Betty both had to have been aware of it. That affair went on for two years. I did a lot of drinkin' and cheatin' and disappearin'.

About the time Josh turned five, things really started going downhill I would get a DWI and go to jail. I would get a DWI and go to treatment. I would get in a fight and wind up in jail. This progressed. It got worse and worse.

One time I went to treatment for five months. It was for mental health and alcohol addiction. So, I was away from home for five months. I was in Fergus Falls at the big hospital. I was sober for most of those five months. I got drunk just once. That meant I had to start treatment all over again. So I was out of my kids' lives for that period. Betty brought the boys to visit me in the hospital. Every time I was so happy to see them.

Finally I was released from treatment. Betty drove over to Fergus to pick me up. On the drive home, Betty stopped and bought a 12-pack of beer. It was like she didn't want me to be sober. It was really weird. She was angry. Betty wasn't happy when I was drinking because I wasn't around. But she wasn't happy when I wasn't drinking because I was around. She wasn't happy when I was working because I wasn't around. She wasn't happy when I wasn't working because we didn't have any money. What was I supposed to do?

**(Left to right) Josh, Betty and Jeremy in about 1989**

We still had some good times. Betty and I could have a lot of fun together. Every now and then we would take off for a weekend together. We would go down to Fargo and stay in a hotel, go to the mall and hang around. My mom would take care of our kids.

Betty had a really caring side. She was affectionate with the boys. She hugged them and kissed them and told them she loved them. She told me she loved me too.

When I became a father, I swore that I would never be like my dad. That mostly meant that I would never hit my kids. I would talk to them. I would be involved. I would spank them but only on the butt. I didn't spank them out of anger. It was more a disciplinary thing for when they did something that was really wrong. I hit Betty one time, and I realized that I was turning into my dad, and I never hit Betty or another woman since.

I did some of the good things that my dad did. My dad played softball with us. We would go camping. I wanted to do things like that with my boys. I wanted to swim with them. Dad taught us all to swim. I let the school teach Jeremy and Josh to swim, but once they learned to swim a little bit, we were in the water together a lot. There was a little swimming hole in Erskine where we would go swimming.

I always tried to be positive with my sons. If they did something wrong, I would tell them, "I love you, but your behavior is out of hand." I remember Jeremy started school, and he came home with his first report card. It was a good report card. But it said there was a little bit of behavior problems. I was so happy with him and his good report card. I told him, "You are doing good in school. You are paying attention. And you've got to settle down a little bit, Jeremy." I went to a parent-teacher conference. I was that involved with my kids. They would tell me how well they were doing, and I would just be really excited.

### Happy times with my boys

My life with the boys was the happiest I had ever been in my life. I would have snowball fights with them. We would make snowmen. We spent a lot of time outside. In the fall of the year when acorns were falling, we would get into acorn fights. All the neighborhood kids would be over in my yard, and they would all be throwing acorns at me. It was a daily thing. I would get off work and come home, and I would be slaughtered by these acorns. A lot

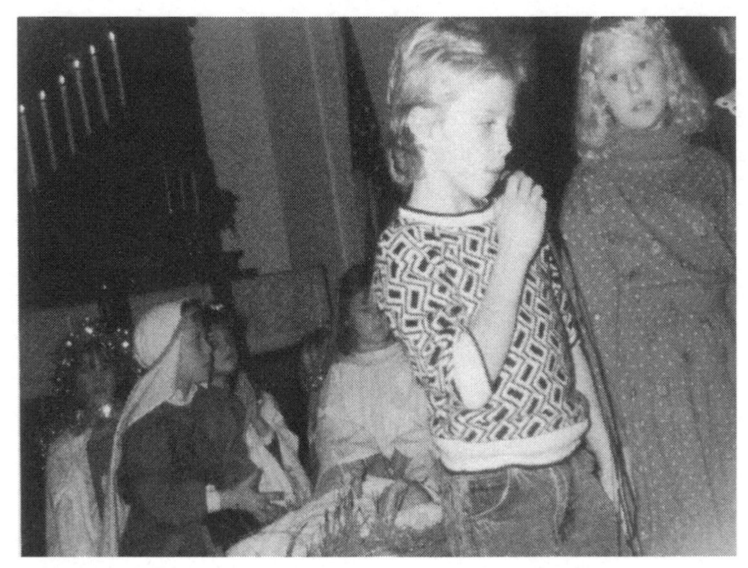

**In the church Christmas pageant Jeremy has the lead role playing Joseph.**

of the neighborhood kids came over to hang out in our yard. We had stuff for kids. We had bicycles and toys.

But they were good kids, my boys. When we went shopping they wouldn't whine and carry on. All I had to do was look at them—give them "the look" and they knew that they better settle down. I never hit 'em. I never screamed and hollered and told them they were stupid and all that. I would say, "You did something really dumb. What could we do to change that?" I wouldn't tell them that they were dumb, because I remembered how it affected me. I had very good rapport with my boys. We would sit down at the dinner table and talk about what was good that was going on in life. What had happened in school? We did that regardless whether Betty was at work or not.

Of course, Christmas was always big. We never had a lot of money to spend on Christmas, but we always had a big Christmas tree. I decorated the house. The kids and I decorated the outside of the house. I had a lot of Christmas lights. I crawled up and made a star in the front window upstairs. I decorated the inside with all different colors. We had garlands all over the place. We really did it up for Christmas. We knew that we didn't have a lot to buy presents, but we always made really good meals. We would get together with my sister and her family and my brother Bill and his family. There would be twenty of us gathered together for a meal every Thanksgiving, Christmas and Easter.

### This Might Be It

Probably the most hopeful job was in 1988 when I got a job at the Thief River Falls Arctic Cat factory making Arctic Cat snowmobiles. It was one of the best-paying jobs in the area. I had good hours. We were living in Erskine at the time. I drove back and forth to Thief River Falls with another guy. By this time I had a number of DWI's so I was no longer driving. Other things were going really well for me.

Betty went to work in the café in the evening working as a waitress. So I was with the boys each evening. I would come home from work. We had a babysitter to cover the 45 minutes from the time that the boys got out of school until I got home. Then it was just me and the boys.

I would take the boys for a walk to see Betty. She was working 7 or 8 blocks away as a waitress at the "Nescafe." About once a week we'd go up and eat supper with her. Josh would always lag a half a block behind us. He was lollygagging around. He had to stop and look at things. He enjoyed himself. He'd stop and look at this. He'd stop and look at that. Jeremy and I would be a half a block ahead. "Josh, quit your lollygagging." He was never in a hurry.

But everybody at Arctic Cat was getting laid off. I took these tests that the company gave me for work in their shipping department. I passed the tests with flying colors. They were ready to transfer me into shipping where the work would be year-round. I was excited. This might be it. This might be the break I needed.

Maybe now my life would straighten out. Everybody else was getting laid off, and I was about to get promoted. Betty was happy.

It was around Thanksgiving time. I went on a drunk and lost the job. I just blew it. I don't know why I went on that drunk. I guess I was just thirsty. I was so obsessed with drinking that I was either drinking, thinking about drinking or thinking about not drinking.

I was drinking a lot of whiskey at the time. In a typical day I drank a quart of whiskey plus a 12-pack of beer. I started drinking once I had this steady job. Within a week I didn't show up for work, and they let me go. Now I couldn't get unemployment, because I had been fired.

### The Christmas miracle

Christmas was approaching, and we had no money. I didn't know what we were going to do. One day I went out to the mailbox, and there was a profit-sharing check from Arctic Cat. I learned that my foreman told the company that she had laid me off – instead of firing me. So, I got the year-end bonus. It was $560. I bought Christmas presents for the kids that year. They were four and six years old at the time. We had a good Christmas because of that.

Josh and I went ice fishing one time. Jeremy was in school. I probably didn't spend as much time with Josh, the second child. But this day Josh and I were out ice fishing. It was cold. We didn't have a fish house. I was using a hand auger drilling a hole in the ice. Josh stuck it out because he liked to fish. When he was five years old, we would go fishing together in the summertime. He could sit there for hours and wait for a fish to bite. He had the patience to do that. Jeremy didn't have the patience. He would sit for two minutes, and if there wasn't a bite, he went off to do other things.

By the time I got the hole drilled through thick ice, it was painfully cold. So Josh and I jumped in the car. We didn't fish.

**Betty and John in the summer of 1990 when their body language says it all.**

We just got in the car and went back to the restaurant where we warmed up with coffee and hot chocolate. I remember how patient he was with me. He watched me drilling that hole. I kept saying, "You OK, Josh?" He said, "I'm OK, Dad. I'm OK. Let's fish." I just loved Josh. He was reassuring me.

### The fight

Betty and I had been married eight years when we got into a fight. I was trying to pay off a fine, working where I could, putting in extra hours where I could. We didn't have physical fights. Our fights were verbal—very verbal. By this time our sexual life was gone.

My brother Bruce and I had been doing a painting job together, and we had earned a bunch of money. We decided to reward ourselves with a good drunk together over at Bruce's house. Betty started phoning me. Bruce lived in McIntosh, and she was in Erskine. She kept calling me telling me to come home. I told her, "Just leave me alone. I'll be home in a little bit." Then she called back and started talking about killing herself. That got my attention.

I said, "Wait a minute. I'll come and help you." So, I took off in my car. When I pulled into our driveway in Erskine, a cop drove in from one way and a second cop drove up from another direction. They arrested me on a DWI. I truly think she set me up—called the cops on me. I wound up getting a DWI, went to jail and got sentenced to a year in the Crookston jail. That was my eigth DWI and sixth DWI in Minnesota.

While in jail they assigned me to work release which means you can work while you're in jail. They let you out in the morning, and you signed a contract saying you'll be back that night. Well, I neglected to go back. I went to work one morning and never returned. I went to Montana. After a few days I was getting ready to return and turn myself in. I wanted to be with my kids. But while I was returning, I got caught in Deadwood, South Dakota. They had a manhunt out for me.

They hauled me back to the main jail in Crookston. I wound up getting additional time for walking out. They could have given me another full year. "Escape" carries one year. But I argued with the judge that it wasn't really an "escape." I said it was a "breach of contract." I argued that they let me go in the morning. I didn't escape. I had signed a contract saying I'd be back every night. I just broke the contract. The judge said, "Well, technically you are right, but I've got to do something. I'll give you 60 more days." So, I was stuck in the main jail in Crookston for a total of 13 months.

The following spring, in the spring of 1991, Betty visited me in jail. She told me she was leaving with the kids. I think she told me in person because she wanted to see the hurt on my face. There wasn't a thing I could do about it. If we had been single, or separated or divorced, it would have been a felony for her to take the kids out of state, but because we were still legally married, she could take the kids anywhere she wanted. I remained stuck behind bars serving out my jail sentence.

**John is alone in 1992 after his release from 13 months in jail.**

THE WORST DAY OF MY LIFE

I loved those boys dearly. When they were taken away from me, it was the worst day of my life. I had experienced some lows before, but this was a new low in my life. She hid the kids from me. Despite my best efforts to find them, I didn't see my boys for years. At the time I had no idea how long it would take to connect with them. I had no idea that I would not see Josh again for 12 years or Jeremy for 17 years.

# 5

# The Good Times

### Trying to find my boys

I had been in jail for 14 months. When I finally got out of jail, it was the beginning of August of 1991, and it was really, really hot out. For months I had been stuck in that jail wondering where my boys were. I figured Betty took the kids to Portland. Her family was there, and I had the address of her mom and dad in Portland. So my plan was to go to Portland to try to find my kids.

But I was stuck in Crookston. I had no money. I didn't have anything except the clothes on my back when I was released from jail. I really had no place to go. But at that time my brother had an apartment downtown over a business, right across the street from the pawn shop. It was a good location—right down the street from the bars. I stayed with Bruce for a couple weeks. I found a job working on a surveying crew holding the story pole. I worked there for a week or so. Then I met Jaybird.

Jaybird was originally from Danbury, Connecticut. He had an East Coast accent. He was about 5'10" with long brown hair, and he always wore his baseball cap backwards. He explained that when you're on a freight train, your hat will blow off unless you have it on backwards. Jaybird was a serious kind of guy. He didn't laugh a whole lot. On the other hand, I joked around a lot. He didn't seem to like the humor. He wanted to be serious and feel sorry for himself. He was alright to hang around with. But if you allowed him to, he could bring you down.

I will say this about Jaybird. He was well geared. He had a backpack with all the gear you needed to ride freight trains and live outside. He had a tarp and everything. I carried nothing but a burrito or a small backpack. I met Jaybird at the mission where he was staying. He got General Assistance with food stamps, but the nun who ran the mission tried to take his food stamps as payment for rent.

I raised cane with her. I told her, "You cannot take somebody's food stamps for rent. It's against the federal law."

She got angry, "I'll call the cops."

That was fine with me. They arrived. They told her, "That's right. You can't take away his food stamps for rent."

Now the nun was really angry. She called me the "spawn of the devil." I had never been called that before. But this argument probably drew Jaybird and me together. We started hanging out.

I talked about getting to Portland. I had not been on a train in almost ten years since before I was married. Jaybird had been riding steadily. He was the expert. He said we should find a "grainer" car. He said they gave a smoother ride than a boxcar. He explained we would find exactly what we needed in Fargo. So, we went to the big railroad yard in Fargo and looked around.

Jaybird explained that the trains in the Fargo railyard were either going east or west. And if you looked at the direction of the three locomotives that pulled the train, you could tell which direction the train was headed. The last thing you needed was to figure out was whether the train was taking the Low Line or the High Line. There was one westbound track leaving Fargo but about 20 miles west of Fargo the lines split. The Low Line took the south fork to the coalfields of Wyoming. The High Line took the north fork to Seattle. If you saw cars that read "Evergreen," that told you it was headed for the High Line because those Evergreen cars were going to Everett, Washington.

We found a grainer and jumped on. Our train stopped every so often. Most of the stops were to let another train pass by. We would pull over onto a siding because there was only one track, and the train going in the opposite direction had to get by us. When the train stopped, we got off, stretched our legs and walked around a little. Sometimes it was only a few minutes but we could wait for as much as two hours.

It was a smooth ride all the way to Libby, Montana. That was a nice little town. We were thirsty so we got off. We found the Libby tramp camp that has been established years ago. At the camp there was a big box covered with a lid. It had been there for years. Jaybird explained that it was part of the tramp code that the box always had a supply of food. So, if you were hungry, there was food there for you. But the honor code called for you to leave some food there.

As we approached Portland, Jaybird and I split company. He went to northern California, and I went to Portland. This was my chance to be reunited with my boys. I found the apartment building. It was a bunch of top and bottom duplexes. I saw their name on the downstairs door. I will call them Ben and Sally Elgin. I knocked on the door. Sally answered the door. She was Betty's mother. She was a blonde, heavy-set woman. She was a woman who really didn't have much good to say about anything. She was kind of a hateful woman. She had mental illness. She had been in and out of the state hospital for many years. When she saw me, she said, "Betty and the boys aren't here. We don't need you around here. We don't need your kind. There are places in downtown Portland for people like you."

So I left. I suspected Betty and the boys were there. I found a light rail track along a line of trees where I could sit and watch the house. It was maybe 50 yards from the house. I sat and watched it. I was there for three, four hours. I had a bottle, so I was drinking to occupy my time. Nobody ever came out of the house. I finally got frustrated and went back downtown.

I wound up meeting a guy named Art at a bar in downtown Portland. We had a few drinks and got acquainted, and then he invited me to come home with him. Art said I could stay with him for a while. That first night he took me across the street to meet some of his drinking friends. They turned out to be a Mormon couple. I will call them Bill and Mary. They were drinking heavily. Then the four of us drank together. Bill was older than Mary—maybe 20 years older. They were decent people, but they were drunk all the time. Each was drinking a half gallon a day.

So for the next several weeks I stayed with Art. During the day I returned to the Elgin place and sat out of sight where I could watch the house. I never saw anyone coming or going.

Each night Art and I would go across the street to drink with Bill and Mary.

Sometimes when we drank together, Bill would pass out. One night Art stayed home, and I was over there drinking with them. Bill passed out, and Mary and I got it on. I was in my early 30's. I was a lot younger than she. I guess she wanted sex with a younger guy. But I think she was attracted to something else. She saw me as a mystery person. I was riding freight trains. I had adventures and stories to tell. I think she was attracted to that. Anyway while we were getting it on, Bill suddenly woke up and caught us.

He kind of freaked out. So, I grabbed my stuff and left. Bill and Mary got into a big fight. Bill moved out, and I moved across the street and stayed with Mary for about three weeks. Mary was heavy-set, but she was really a good looking woman. Mary was about 25 years older than I.

I was still going out to the Elgin house to see if I could see my boys. Mary offered to help me. She offered to pretend she was a social worker and make a call on Ben and Sally Elgin and see if she could locate my kids.

But then Bill got back into the picture, and I decided that discretion was the best part of valor and left. By this time Betty's brothers started threatening me. Her brothers were bad news. I later learned that one brother was sent to life in prison for shooting a cop. Another brother was schizophrenic, and when he thought someone was messing with his wife, he shot him. The whole family had mental issues. They were crazy and dangerous. If I persisted in trying to see the boys, I could wind up dead. I had been staying in Portland for months without ever seeing my boys. I had lost the roof over my head. It was always raining in Portland. It was time to move on.

### Falling in love with riding a freight train

My brother Bruce introduced me to riding freight trains before I was married, and it was love at first sight. It was what I was looking for. On that first ride on a freight train, I was with Bruce and Bufflee leaving Denver and heading for Minnesota. It was a July evening. We got on a boxcar where we had a great big picture window—the open door of the boxcar. It was a beautiful summer evening. We watched the trees and rivers go by. We saw antelope bounding across the plains.

I had an immediate sense of freedom. Nobody could touch me. We were moving. We knew we were on the move. It was a great feeling. Sometimes you didn't know exactly where you were going, but you were on the move. I also had a sense of excitement. This was a new adventure for me. I had never felt this before. Jumping on a freight train was a new rush for me.

I have seen a lot of the United States from coast to coast, riding freight trains. It has been a life of adventure. I still remember some perfect train rides—like the time I rode from White Fish to Havre, Montana. It was a beautiful day—sunny, probably 75 degrees. I had everything that I needed—a little acid, a case of beer, a jug of whiskey, a bag of pot, a bedroll, a jug of water, and a good suspense novel. I think it was Stephen King. Riding a train was the most exciting thing I had ever experienced. I liked almost everything about it. I liked that "clickity clack, clickity clack" sound. The train was rocking back and forth. It was soothing. I was perfectly content. I remember going through the Badlands the first time, and I stared at all the different colored rocks. I was just fascinated. When I got back to Minnesota, I knew I was going to do this again.

Sometimes I was alone, and I liked that—the solitude, the quiet, the peace. Other times I was with some traveling companions, and I usually enjoyed the comradery. You instantly had something in common with another person riding the same freight train. When you were rolling down the track, you were cut off from everybody. No one could harass you. You were off in your own little world.

My brother Bruce taught me one of the songs of freight train riders. It goes, "Oh, hand me down my walking cane. Oh, hand me down my walking cane. Oh, hand me down my walking cane. I'm gonna leave on the midnight train. All my sins are takin' away." It has many verses. I think perhaps Woody Guthrie wrote it back when he was riding trains. We sang away.

Most of the people riding freight trains were colorful characters. On the road everyone had a road name. Either you picked your own or someone named you. My road name was "Fritz." There was "Road Runner" who was always on the go. There was a couple who went by "Jack" and "Jill." Another couple was called "Dog" and "Cat" because they fought all the time. There were a few women who rode freight trains—not many. One colorful woman was "Dirty Donna." She kept herself dirty and smelly so men wouldn't get too friendly with her. There was Santa Claus (who had a big belly and a white beard). One guy was called "Twin Stacks." He was going through a sex change. He was getting hormones shots that gave him big boobs. I don't think anybody harassed him or was cruel to him. But we thought he was a little weird, and we avoided him. Another guy we called "Tornado," because his real name was Gale.

Almost all were alcoholics, and many had mental illness, but there was a spirit of acceptance that made friendships possible. You learned the location of tramp camps. Some freight train riders looked for missions when they got off the train, but I was part of the hard core that looked for tramp camps and stayed outside.

I flew a sign, got some money in my pocket and returned to the camp with some food and booze. We built a campfire and had a party. We shared what we had. That was one of the rules of the road. "Everyone shares."

**Both the "twin stack" (above) and the "grainer" (below) have a narrow ledge front and rear where you can ride.**

With experience I learned some of the important tricks of the trade. I learned how to figure out more or less where the train was going before I jumped on. I learned what kind of car to jump on. Forget coal cars. You could never get rid of that coal dust. I started with boxcars but soon learned that the best rides are in "twin stacks" and "grainers." Both had platforms at the end of the car where you could sit, stand or lie down, and most important the ride was much smoother than a boxcar. Sometimes you found yourself riding a car with a bad bearing. The car would bump every time the wheel rotated go. It would go "clunk, clunk, clunk." You learned to find another car.

There was a sort of club that some tramps joined. It was officially called the FTRA—the "Freight Trainer Riders of America." Originally it was started by a bunch of homeless Vietnam vets. They sometimes called themselves the "Fuck the Reagan Administration." They even wore distinctive scarves such as a bandana with a ring around it. In my experience these guys were often violent. They got in fights with each other, and they weren't very friendly to outsiders. I stayed away from them. I preferred to ride with people I could trust or else ride by myself.

I learned about the essentials to take with me on a freight train: Start with a case of beer and a jug of liquor such as a half-gallon of vodka. Then bring some acid and some weed to make hand-rolled cigarettes. Finally, a jug of water is very important. I learned that the best jug is a used plastic jug that originally contained orange juice. For some reason those jugs are industrial strength. They last for months. You fill it with water and throw it unto the railroad car, and it bounces. It doesn't burst. Then you bring a bedroll, some dehydrated food and some road flares. Of course, you always keep a magic marker in your pocket. You can find cardboard almost anywhere and create a sign.

If you want to heat up some ramen noodles, dehydrated potatoes or coffee, you pour it into a beer can of water and heat the water up by lighting a road flare. Within five minutes the water will be boiling. I liked to read, so I always brought along a book. When you are settled on a good car, with everything you need, rolling across the countryside, it is a very good feeling.

Of course, you would need a little money to buy booze and some food, but that wasn't hard to figure out. You flew a sign, and you usually brought in $50 per day. That was plenty for a day's worth of booze and food. Or sometimes you found a dumpster behind a restaurant with plenty of food. I remember the first time I ate out of a dumpster. I was 18 years old and on the streets in San Diego. It was hard for me the first time. What will people think of me? I was embarrassed, but it got easier and easier. Pretty soon I wasn't embarrassed at all. I would even climb into the dumpster and stand up, eating and waving at people as they stared at me. I had the best luck with Kentucky Fried Chicken places. I learned that you could go to the back door of any Kentucky Fried Chicken restaurant and ask for some food, and they would always give you something. I heard a rumor that it was a policy started by Colonel Sanders himself.

But you could also dig into their dumpster. You would often find a whole bunch of fried chicken—perfectly good—that had been thrown out at closing time. One time in Bend, Oregon, we found a Kentucky Fried Chicken dumpster with more food than we knew what to do with. Once when I was living on the streets in Los Angeles I found one particular Kentucky Fried Chicken restaurant where the employees boxed up the left-over food and placed the boxes on top of the dumpster for our convenience.

Finally, there was a fringe benefit of riding freight trains. Yes, people sometimes called us tramps or hoboes, but we were also celebrities. We were mystery people. Some suspected that we had seen places and experienced things that they could hardly imagine. At times we were treated like rock stars—celebrities. It was surprising the way some people were drawn to us—high school kids, college kids, tourists, all kinds of people.

### "We have more than we need"

One day I was with Tornado and RC in Fargo, North Dakota. We decided it was time to leave Fargo and head west. I was on my way to Oregon. I knew that the first stop would be Minot for a crew change. There was always a crew change in no more than eight hours, because eight hours was the most an engineer was allowed to drive the train.

It was a beautiful, beautiful summer day—probably 80 degrees with a nice breeze. Along came this freight train. We jumped on. The wind was cooling. It was getting late at night when we arrived in Minot. We were riding on different cars, so when the train slowed, I jumped off my car. I didn't know if Tornado and RC got off or not. But I was committed. I wanted to stop in Minot. For the moment I was alone.

It was the middle of the night, but it was still nice out.

There wasn't a soul around. I didn't know where Tornado and RC were, so I camped out right there for the night. I found a bridge right near the Amtrak station. I crawled up underneath. It was dark. I knew I would stay dry under that bridge. I had my "burrito" with me. The burrito was my bedroll with a change of clothes rolled up inside. The bedroll was wrapped inside a small tarp. You always wrapped everything in a tarp in case of rain. That tarp and that bedroll could be your life line to keep you from freezing.

The next morning I woke up to a sunny, beautiful morning but I could tell it was going to be a hot day. I hadn't had anything to eat for about 24 hours, and my jug of vodka was almost empty. I needed to get to the center of town, but that meant walking up a long hill to downtown Minot. It must have been two miles long. That's where I had to go for a good intersection to fly my sign, get something to eat or drink and look for Tornado and RC. The hill was gradual, but it went up and up forever. I had to get to the crest of that hill. I was carrying my burrito with me, and it was getting heavy. I felt like throwing it away. As I marched up that hill it was getting heavier and heavier. I was getting hot, thirsty and tired.

I finally got to the top of the hill and saw a good spot to fly a sign. Who was there? Tornado. There was no sign of RC, but there was my buddy, Tornado. Tornado was tall and thin. He was a "home guard" guy in Fargo. If someone was homeless but stayed on the streets in their hometown, we called them the "home guard." Tornado had never been out of Fargo until this trip when I persuaded him to join me riding a freight train. This was his first freight train ride. I was going to take him with me to the West Coast and show him the ropes. He was all excited about seeing the world with me. He was about my age—late 40's. Tornado was very easy going. He laughed a lot. He was a wonderful guy to be around. If he had something you needed, he would give it to you.

I saw him standing there leaning into the passenger side of a nice looking Ford Explorer talking to the driver through the open window. When I walked up, I saw that the driver was a woman. In fact, she was a black woman. That was a surprise because in Minot, North Dakota you don't see many black people—men or women.

Tornado smiled and waved for me to join him talking through the window. She was a young woman, maybe 35 years old, well dressed and well spoken. She didn't have a "black accent." If anything, she had a Minnesota accent. She was a good-looking lady. I am wondering what is she doing in Minot? Then it hit me—the Air Force Base. She has something to do with the Minot Air Force Base.

Now there were two of us peering through the window at her. She asked, "What do you guys need?"

I said, "We need food."

She said, "Jump in."

We looked at each other for a second, and then we jumped in. Tornado got in the front seat with her, and I got into the back seat of this big Ford Explorer. She drove down the highway a little, then made a U-turn and headed back to the grocery store. The three of us walked into the store together. I pulled out a grocery cart, and we were wondering what to do. Tornado and I looked at each other. We were both uncomfortable.

We just stood there—almost paralyzed. Tornado told her, "We don't know what to do here."

She said, "Just go buy something."

He asked, "How much do you want us to spend?"

She said, "I don't care. Just go get yourself some food."

I was standing there with the cart. I still didn't want to start putting groceries in the cart. Neither did Tornado. He started wandering around. We had no clue what to do. No one had ever done this to us before. I had been flying signs for years, but nobody had ever taken me to a grocery store and told me to start shopping. I still didn't know what to do.

She noticed our holding back, and she asked us, "What do you guys eat?"

I said, "Ramen noodles and all kinds of dehydrated foods that we can mix with hot water. We don't carry cans or glass jars because they get heavy."

She started throwing packages of Ramen noodles in the cart, then some bread, and next some dehydrated potatoes. I was pushing the cart, and she was throwing stuff into the cart. I didn't know how much she was going to spend. She just kept throwing stuff in and throwing stuff in—lunch meat, cheese. I was thinking this is getting expensive. I was amazed at this woman. Who is this woman to be doing this? Maybe she's a Christian. People don't do this.

We got to the check-out counter. The total bill came to $68. Tornado and I were there with our backpacks, and we stuffed the food into those two backpacks. Between our two backpacks, we bagged all the food. I always carried my backpack when I went to a grocery store.

By this time other customers in the check-out line were staring at the three of us. Probably they were wondering, "What is this crazy lady doing with these two tramps?" I am sure we made an odd combination—especially in Minot, North Dakota. When we were done in the grocery store, she said, "Well, do you need something to drink?"

Tornado and I looked at each other. By now I was shaking a little bit with the beginning of my usual withdrawal symptoms, and I said, "Well, yeah."

"OK, let's go to the liquor store."

Now, I was really surprised. I figured that she was a Christian woman, and I never thought she would buy me booze. But she walked us over to the liquor store which is connected to the grocery store.

By this time I was getting a little more comfortable, so I quickly grabbed a 12-pack of beer. But she said, "No, you need more than that. "

So, I exchanged the 12-pack for a case, and right away she said, "Take two of them."

Then she said, "Why don't you get yourself a bottle too?"

"OK" I grabbed a bottle of vodka.

We checked out and she handed the cashier another $30.

We brought everything out to the car. Now we thought we were done. We've got groceries, beer and vodka. Then she said, "You guys smoke, don't you?"

I asked "What?"

"You guys smoke, don't you?"

"Well, yeah."

"Let's go over to the gas station over here. They've got cheap cigarettes." She bought us a carton of cigarettes.

I was saying to myself, "OK, lady. What's going on here? What do you want out of us?" I couldn't figure out why she was doing all this. What is she getting out of this? We got back into the car with the cigarettes. Now we had booze, we had food, cigarettes. We were high styling it.

Next she asked us, "Now where do you want to go?"

Tornado said he was camping under a nearby bridge. She said, "Show me the way. I'll give you a ride down there."

As we were getting out of the car and loading up everything, I was thanking her profusely. She just waved me off. She said, "Never mind. We can afford this. My husband is an officer in the Air Force, and we have more than we need." She gave us each a $100 bill and drove off.

### My lady friend Linda

One day I got off the train in Missoula, Montana. It was a beautiful mountain town. I was alone as usual. It was August. When you are in Missoula, you can look up into the mountains and see where they had clear cut all the trees. There was a big

"M" up on this mountain. I had never been to Missoula before, but I found the mission that served meals. Missions are usually close to the railroad. I went into the mission to grab a bite, and I met this tall skinny kid.

He called himself "Snappy." It wasn't important to learn someone's real name. He was just Snappy. I think he was from Ohio. I never knew his story. He didn't share a lot about himself. He was closed off. He was younger—maybe 25 years old. He had dark hair. Sometimes he acted like a clown. He was very thin. Snappy was so thin he could rip out the bottom of a plastic grocery bag, pull it over him and wear the bag like a tank top shirt. Then he would go out and fly a sign. People would think, "Poor guy can't even afford a shirt." Within a few weeks Snappy began to follow me around like a little puppy dog. I was older than he and a lot bigger. I think he counted on me taking care of business if we got in a tough spot.

Snappy had already met a gal called "Dirty Donna." She rode freight trains by herself which is unusual. She kept herself filthy in order to keep men away. Donna was a blonde gal from the mountains of North Carolina, so she had a Southern accent. Snappy and I saw Dirty Donna as well as another girl—Linda. Linda was a Native American wearing blue jeans, a T shirt and a baseball cap. She was short and thin and had brown, shoulder-length hair. I thought she was attractive in her own way. She was a good looking girl with a nice enough body. I didn't know how she dared to be hanging out here alone. She had a missing front tooth, and she had a scar on her right check. But she had this beautiful smile, and I liked her right away. She had brown eyes, and one eye had a blue speck. I called it a floater. I found her attractive. I immediately felt protective of her.

I later learned that she was from Pine Ridge, South Dakota. Both Linda and her brother were adopted by a white family in Minnesota, and she was raised as a white girl. She was trying to get back to her roots—trying to find out about Native culture. But recently she had been drinking a lot and riding freight trains. She had a hard life. She had been with a guy, but he deserted her in Missoula, Montana. She had no bedroll, no backpack, no money, nothing to eat or drink. She didn't even have a purse or any identification. All she had were the clothes on her back. We all lived outside, but I soon learned that she went to gas station bathrooms and kept herself clean.

We found a liquor store, a grocery store and a place to fly a sign. We got some vodka, my preferred drink, and we got acquainted over a little vodka. Me being the hero that I am, I told her that she could hang out with us. By this time Dirty Donna had disappeared.

**This is the beautiful Rattlesnake Creek where Linda and I enjoyed the night.**

So the three of us—Snappy, Linda and I—set up camp along a beautiful creek—the Rattlesnake Creek on the east edge of Missoula. The highway bridge for I-90 is not far away. It was a beautiful spot. We were camped under a huge pine tree. The Rattlesnake Creek was so clear you could drink it. The creek was right there. I could hear it babbling. You could see that tramps had camped there before. It was an obvious place to set up a camp. But at this time we had the camp to ourselves.

We had a nice grassy area, and our camp was hidden in a little hollow where nobody could see us. It was very private. I had my coffee travel mug with me. I just dipped the mug into the creek and scooped up a cup of delicious cold drinking water. I unfolded my bedroll and invited her to sleep on it, and I slept beside her. Life was looking pretty good at the moment. I had a woman that I could hang out with, and I could bring in enough money each day flying a sign so that I could keep us supplied with booze.

I should explain that my mother taught me to treat all women as a gentleman would treat any lady. Of course, it was the exact opposite of the role my father had played. So, that first night I slept on my part of my bedroll, and she slept on the other. I didn't touch her. I think she might have been a little surprised.

I remember that first morning with Linda. We woke up, and it was a beautiful, sunny morning. I made a sign and Linda joined me while I flew my sign. We took turns—first Linda and I together, and then Snappy would take our place. I would use a sign that read either "Homeless. Please help us eat today" or just "Heading home." With either sign we did real well. You always made more money when you were standing there as a couple. People would stop, and they would hand money over to me. In the meantime Linda was having a good time. She would talk and laugh and kid around. People would see us together, and they probably thought, "These people are OK." We didn't act like we were sad so that people would feel sorry for us. Instead, Linda and I just had a good time together.

We did pretty well. We were bringing in $50 - $60 a day. Once again Linda and I slept side by side in my bedroll, and again I didn't touch her. I was tempted, of course, but I was also patient. I didn't try to have sex with her. I showed Linda that she would be safe around me. I think Linda was amazed. Here was a tramp, and he was not taking advantage of her.

On the third night she started snuggling up close to me, rubbing against me. She came on to me. We had sex that night alongside the Rattlesnake Creek. It was wonderful.

This was our life for the next two or three weeks. Linda and I were really digging each other. Linda cared for me. She was upbeat all the time. She kept me positive.

The three of us stayed in Missoula for a couple of weeks, but then it was time to move on. People became accustomed to us standing at the same street corner day after day with the same sign. I was still flying those same signs, "Homeless. Please help us eat today" or "Heading home" but we were still hanging around. It was getting old. Our money was drying up.

Snappy, Linda and I decided to head west toward Spokane. The first thing I did was buy three half gallons of wine. I stuffed them in my back pack. We planned to hop on a train that evening, and we found ourselves down by the mission. It was starting to get dark, and this guy walked out of the mission. He walked up to Linda and started harassing her. He was a big guy—about my size—6' - maybe 235 pounds. He grabbed her arm, and she tried to pull away.

That's all it took. I grabbed his arm and pushed him away. Apparently he wasn't used to being challenged. He took a round house swing at me. He was big and strong, but he wasn't an experienced fighter. He hadn't been living outside where you have to be ready to take care of yourself. I was pretty big and strong, but I was also experienced. I had been in plenty of fights. I leaned back and avoided his wild right, and then I stepped forward and threw a hard punch with my big right hand. I caught him square in the face. He went down. I hit pretty hard. I kicked him a couple times. That's all it took. He realized that I could kick his ass. I let him get up, and he took off running. I thought that was the end of it. "Fine, just leave my woman alone."

So, Snappy, Linda and I were standing there by the mission, waiting for the train. It was getting darker. The train was due any minute. But suddenly the cops arrived.

They said, "You. Come here."

"OK"

"Let's see some ID."

We gave them our ID's. They returned to their cop car. They

ran our IDs. No problems. Now they walked back and said to me, "You just assaulted a man. We need to take you to jail."

I shrugged, "Fine. Let's go."

I got into the police car and was driven to jail with Snappy and Linda standing there watching the car drive off. I spent the night in jail, and I was due to appear in court the next morning. I didn't know what to expect. Probably Snappy and Linda would be gone, and I might get a jail sentence of a week or a month. The next morning I was dressed in the jailhouse orange coveralls and taken into the courtroom. I looked around, and the first people I saw in the courtroom were Snappy and Linda. I thought "Wow. These people really care." I was kind of surprised because at that point in my life it seemed like nobody really cared about me. I know it was Linda—she probably dragged Snappy there. They learned that I was going to appear in court in the morning, so when I was taken into the courtroom, they were waiting.

The judge sized up the situation. "Mr. Fritz, there is something a little strange here. This fellow that you assaulted yesterday, also got into a fight with someone else the day before. I'm going to give you a fine of $300 and give you six months to pay the fine." He banged his gavel. He was giving me what we call a "get-out-of-town ticket." He figured out that this other guy was the real trouble maker.

I was released from jail early that afternoon. As they were releasing me, I joked with the jailers. I had been in plenty of jails, and I had learned that the best way to deal with jail was to cooperate and joke around. So, as I was being released, I said something like, "I really don't like your accommodations here, Sir. I want to file a formal complaint about the food." I smiled. They laughed and told me to get going. Jailers can be very decent. They often have to deal with angry people, so they appreciate it when someone comes in and jokes around.

Both Linda and Snappy were at the jail door for me. The jailer returned my big green Army duffel pack. Lo and behold, my three half-gallons of wine were still there in the backpack. We assumed that the cops would empty out my wine. Linda offered me a drink from her jug of vodka. That vodka was just what I needed. By this time I was starting to shake with withdrawal symptoms.

That evening we hopped on a grainer car to Spokane. I was so happy. I was out of jail, I had those three jugs of wine, we were headed for Spokane and I was with my girlfriend. I couldn't wait. I guess she couldn't either. We had sex right there in the middle of the day on the platform of this freight car. That was fine until our train slowed to a crawl for an intersection. As we inched past a railroad crossing there was a line of cars, and everyone was staring at Linda and me. I didn't know what else to do, so I waved.

Linda was great company. She was always chatting. She was pretty happy. She liked to drink. She liked me. She had this cute expression that she said almost every day. It could be morning, afternoon or evening, but she looked up at me and smiled and said, "Is it time for a little nip?"

Of course I said, "Sure, Linda, let's have a little drink." Linda and I traveled together, and slowly things began to get more serious. Things were never perfect. When she got drunk on vodka, she was often a mean drunk. She would want to fight me. She would swing and kick. I had to hold her off. I think she had two problems with me. First, I was white, and she had some underlying rage against white people. Second, I think she was afraid of getting too close to me or anyone else. I think she was afraid that she would get hurt.

But Linda and I decided to go back home to Minnesota and see if we could sort things out. Maybe we could make this work. As soon as we got back to Minnesota, I was thrown into detox four times in two weeks. I was put in detox for three days and released for a day or so, and returned again for another three days, released, and quickly returned. Then the county sent me to a treatment center in Fergus Falls. In the meantime Linda was staying at my father's place in McIntosh. She got a good job working at a nursing home.

The people who owned the nursing home had a trailer in back that we could rent. I was in treatment for 2 ½ months. I had plenty of time to think. I began thinking, "Maybe we can settle down here in McIntosh—at least for the winter and see how it goes." I had been sober all that time, and I was going to try to stay sober, settle down with Linda and begin a new life. Then I was released from the halfway house, and she drove over to pick me up. I bravely announced "I'm not going to drink."

She brought along a pint of vodka and immediately offered it to me. She said, "Oh, it's time for a little nip. We don't have to get drunk all the time." By the time we got to North Dakota—just 22 miles away—I had finished that bottle. She didn't want to sober up, and she didn't want me to be sober.

### I always had my credit card

Once I was homeless I quickly learned that one of the survival skills for living on the streets of a strange town was a magic marker and a cardboard sign. I first learned about flying a sign in 1992 after failing to connect with my boys. At that time, these homemade cardboard signs were new. I saw them for the first time in Las Vegas. People were just running over each other trying to give us money. It was nothing to make a couple hundred dollars a day. That was the early days of these signs.

A little while later, I was in Salt Lake with two friends, James and Smoke, and they taught me about how to "fly a sign" as they called it. James said he would get a black magic marker and a piece of cardboard from a dumpster. He would write "Please help me eat today." Then he would draw the "Jesus fish." The idea was to appeal specifically to Christians. They would see this Jesus fish, and they would be more likely to give money. You stood at a traffic light or stop sign where people have to stop—the more traffic the better. One of the best spots is on the entrance ramp to a freeway where people are stopped and have to wait to enter.

James advised me, "Never put anything about work on your sign. If you do, people will expect you to work for them." I followed James' advice, and my first sign was "Please help me eat today." I was surprised. It worked. People stopped, rolled down the window and reached out to hand me money.

That was my standard sign: "Please help me eat today." I quickly learned the importance of holidays. Christmas time was the best. I just wrote "Merry Christmas" on my sign. If you were really creative, you used red and green markers. My lady friend Linda used to make some really creative signs. She would make these signs in blues and greens and reds with fancy artwork on them. They worked. Of course if you were standing with Linda then almost everything worked. For a while a friend lent us his dog. The dog was a mutt named "Lipps." He had some German Shepherd in him, but he never barked. He was about two feet tall, brown in color. He was supposed to be a camp watchdog, but he never barked. He was no protection whatsoever. He was one of these mutts that didn't look like any other dog. I would be standing there with Linda, holding Lipps on a leash. That was the perfect combination. A lot of people stopped for us.

At Easter time I wrote "Happy Easter" and drew a Jesus fish. On Fourth of July, I would draw fireworks and write "Happy Fourth of July." At Thanksgiving, I wrote "Happy Thanksgiving." But Christmas was always the best holiday.

On November 12, Veterans' Day, I wrote "Homeless Vet." That was a sign that could be controversial. It could create an emotional reaction. One year I was flying this sign on November 12. A guy was driving a car that read "Veteran's Administration," and he stopped. He was a little angry with me. He demanded to see my military service card. So, I showed him my ID from the time I was in the Navy. He scowled, "OK. I can see you really are a vet. I'll give you twenty bucks for your sign."

I asked, "Why do you want my sign?"

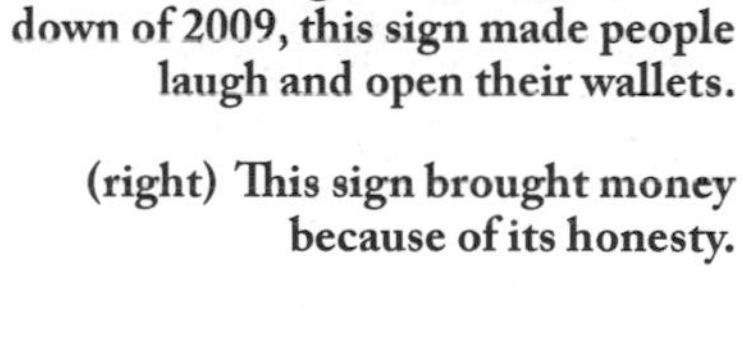
**(above) During the economic meltdown of 2009, this sign made people laugh and open their wallets.**

**(right) This sign brought money because of its honesty.**

He growled, “I don’t want your sign. I just want to get it off the street. It’s an offense to the VA.” I knew what he meant. In fact, I had sometimes taken away a guy’s sign and ripped it up when I found out that he was flying something that was a lie.

I liked to be creative with my signs. I used “Heading home.” Everyone seems to be touched by someone who is trying to go home. A similar sign was “Going to see my Mom. Need help.” That worked. I would get offers of a ride as well as gifts of cash.

A couple others that worked for a while were: “Traveling broke” or “Trying to get home for Christmas.” But I paid attention to other signs and was always looking for a creative twist that could increase my odds of getting money. Once I saw an oversized sign that read, “I need wine.” I burst out laughing. I began writing that on my sign, and it usually produced enough cash to get drunk on. On Friday and Saturday nights I tended to use: “Why lie? I need a beer.” It worked pretty well. Most people gave you a disgusted look, but a good minority gave you money because you were being honest.

I got really creative one day and printed out, “Will work for sex.” I was sitting there looking at my sign, when a cop saw it. He warned me. "You hold that up, and I'll arrest you for soliciting." I guess that sign was too creative.

My favorite sign was one I used here in St. Paul during the 2008-2009 financial melt-down. It said, "Wall Street Bailout." I got a lot of smiles and laughs. A lot of fancy cars like BMW's stopped and gave me money.

### A Good Party

Most of us who rode a freight train just lived to party. Any occasion was a good excuse for a party. We wanted to live from one party to the next. The focus of every party was getting drunk. Sometimes there was a campfire. Sometimes there was singing. Once in a while there was decent food. Many times there was story telling. Occasionally there was some sex. But there was always drinking.

Homemade booze was always a cause for celebration. We called it hooch. In Fargo I had these two buddies, John and Wayne. John had served a life sentence in Indiana for killing his wife. He caught her in bed with another man, and he killed her. He was about 25 years older than me. I was about 33, and he was almost 60. He was released after serving 28 years of his life sentence. Wayne was even older—in his 60's. John had a camp. He had permission to camp about 50 yards behind this business that was located right along the railroad tracks. The business owner had been robbed so many times, he was happy to have us hanging around there. John was established there. He had built himself a shack out of plywood. Soon Wayne and I moved into his camp.

John bragged about his homemade tomato wine. He said he had learned to make it in prison and claimed it was the best drink in the world. He promised to make some for us. Wayne and I were skeptical. John got a five gallon bucket and filled it two-thirds full of very ripe tomatoes. Then he added sugar and yeast before setting it aside to cure for a week.

John was all excited. He was proud of his wine. After a week it was clear liquid—not red juice as you might expect. He had a beer can, and he had removed its top with a P38. That's an army can opener that will remove the entire top of a beer can. Now the beer can became a cup. He dipped his beer can in the pail, took a long swallow of his tomato wine and announced, "That's good stuff, boys."

Wayne refused to touch it. It was Sunday morning, and we were out of money and out of booze. I looked at it. It smelled nasty, but I knew John was proud of it. I didn't want to hurt his feelings. I have to admit I had nothing else to drink, and I was starting to get the shakes. "OK, John, I'll drink this with you." I scooped my beer can in there and took a drink. It was nasty.

John said, "This is good stuff."

I said, "John, this tastes like shit." I can't even describe what it really tasted like. But it was nasty. That didn't stop me. I took another drink and another, and pretty soon I got drunk. It took care of my shakes. I used to get really bad shakes. I drank rubbing alcohol if necessary to get rid of the shakes.

One of our best parties was a birthday party for Beam-me-up-Scotty. It was August in Libby, Montana. The weather was really nice. There was a lot of sunshine. We were in the mountains near Glacier National Park. I was with Jaybird, and when we got off the train, we walked into town.

We met these three guys, and immediately I knew that they were riding freight. You can tell by the way they are dressed—how they carry themselves. We shared a bottle with them. They were Beam-me-up-Scotty, Road Runner and another guy.

They had a camp along Libby Creek. It was just beautiful. The water was crystal clear and ice cold. We are sitting there drinking together, and Scotty was bummed out. He announced that it was his birthday. I had $200 stashed in my wallet. I knew that I really needed this money, but I had new friends here. Finally I burst out, "Scotty, I've got $100. Let's have a party."

Immediately he brightened up. We went into town, got a shopping cart and filled it with cases of beer, bottles of wine, a jug of vodka and then pushed it back about a half mile until we got near our camp. We unloaded the cart and carried all the stuff down into our camp. It was afternoon, and we were all drinking, talking and laughing. Pretty soon Jaybird, Road Runner and another guy made another trip back to town to buy more booze. They returned without Jaybird, but they had more booze. Jaybird had spit on a cop when asked what he was doing. He was in jail for the moment. But they brought along three girls who wanted to party with the tramps. They were good looking girls. I kept wondering, "What are these girls coming into a tramp camp for?" They were old enough to drink. I think they were excited about meeting some tramps.

There was one real good looking blonde that I was trying to impress. I dove into the creek. Of course I was drunk. The creek was pure melted glacier water and so cold that it took my breath away. I couldn't breathe. I would have drowned if Scotty had not pulled me out and let me dry out for a while.

### Enjoying celebrity

One day I hitchhiked from Klamath Falls down to Weed. California. I found beauty wherever I went. Here I could see Mt. Shasta. They called it a double-barreled volcano because it had two stacks. We pulled into this little town of Weed. I got out of the car. I had a few dollars in my pocket. I went to find a liquor store. It was a little, tiny town, and I saw Jaybird. I thought, "Cool. I've got my partner back."

Jaybird and I were walking down the street, and there was this girl. She had brown hair. She was short and chubby. She was carrying a bottle of wine—Mad Dog Wine. I said, "Hey, give us some of that wine." The three of us sat alongside a building drinking her wine. She started picking wild mint that was growing right there, and she explained about wild mint. She started talking to us. She wanted to know what we were about. She lived in this small town, and we were mystery men to her. We had done things she could only dream about. In her eyes we were celebrities.

"Where are you guys from?"

We were passing the bottle around for all three of us. I said, "Minnesota."

"What's your name?"

"I'm Fritz, and this is Jaybird."

"What are you doing out here?"

"Well, we're riding a freight train."

I was in my early 30's and she would have been in her late 20's. She was boisterous, loud. The three of us emptied her bottle, and she said, "I'll get some more wine." She came back with another bottle.

So, we all walked across the freeway, and found a spot under some big trees—a nice camp spot. Jaybird and I decided that this is where we could camp for the night.

She said, "Gee, this is a nice place. I live here, and I've never been here."

Anyway we opened that new bottle, and we just bull-shitted back and forth and finished that second bottle. Now we started teasing her, "Show us your tits!" She said, "Show me your nuts." It was hilarious.

Well, we finished that second bottle. I offered to get a third bottle. I asked her, "Where is the liquor store?" She gave me directions. "Go back to the freeway, walk three blocks down and it's there on the right." When I returned, she and Jaybird were getting it on.

I waited while they finished up, and then we started drinking that third bottle of wine. The next thing you know, she's hanging on to me. The three of us carried on for a while, joked and talked. She told us she had a boyfriend, but they were fighting all the time and she was sick of him. She said she was going to move out of here. It was just a little town.

I rolled out my bedroll, and she lay down with me. Well, we did what men and women do at that age. Then we fell asleep. In the middle of the night, she nudged me and said, “I’m cold.” Well, to me that means, “Let’s do it. Let’s make love again.” So we did.

The next morning she got up and shouted, “I partied with the tramps.” She was just thrilled with it. Then she left.

### High Stylin’ with my cell phone

It was the spring of 2006. I was on the Nicollet Mall, and this guy handed me a cell phone. In fact, he handed me two phones. I had no credit history, and I was drunk at the time. He had to know that I was drunk. I had my backpack on. This guy talked me into buying a phone. He was a young black guy. He was well dressed. He was a very smooth talker. He started filling out the paperwork before I even said I wanted one.

I knew about texting at the time. My girlfriend Patty was texting. He said that I got free texting. Cool. One phone had 500 minutes and free texting. I was thinking, “This is cool. I will give the texting phone to Patty, and I will keep the other.” Patty was living in St. Paul, and sometimes I stayed with her—off and on. She had her sister living with her.

I decided it was time for me to go to Oregon. I geared up. I went to the North Yards by the East River Road in Minneapolis. I called her on my new cell phone. I was sitting in the North Yards and I said, “Well, Patty, I’m just about to get on a train so you won’t hear from me for a while.

“OK. I’ll talk to you when you get back.”

I jumped a train to go west. I was drunk, and I passed out and didn’t wake up until the train arrived in Fargo. The train stopped, and I bailed off.

I phoned Patty again, “Well, I’m in Fargo.”

“What are you going to do?”

“What do you think I’m going to do. I’m going to fly a sign

and get some money in my pocket." We talked a little bit more. She asked about the weather. We just made small talk mainly.

Then I jumped on a train heading for Minot. The train stopped somewhere out in the middle of North Dakota. Well, here is an opportunity to make a phone call. I called Patty again. She had never been to North Dakota. I described the rolling hills and the emptiness. There was nothing around for miles. Meanwhile I was sitting alongside this freight train waiting for it to take off again.

The train started up again, and pretty soon we were in Havre, Montana. Now my phone went dead. So, I went to a McDonald's and asked, "Can you charge my phone for me?"

"Sure enough."

From then on I knew that I could stop at a bar or a McDonald's and charge my phone. Now I was flying a sign, and I phoned Patty again. When I realized what I was doing, I put my phone away. "How can you be asking for money while you are standing there with a cell phone in your hand?"

I soon got back on a train and made it to Portland, and once again I tried to find my children. I thought I knew where they were, but it didn't work out. Now I was really depressed, so I called Patty, and she cheered me up. She told me that I could always come back to Minnesota. I always had a place to stay with her. Anyway, I made more phone calls all the way back to Minnesota. I called my sister, Bev.

"Where are you at?" she asked

"I'm sitting by a freight train in the middle of Montana."

"Well, how are you calling?"

"I've got a cell phone, Bev."

"You do? Where did you get that?"

"Oh, I got it in the Cities."

"Oh, you can stay in touch with us now."

"Yes, Bev, I will. Well, the train is getting ready to leave. I gotta go."

As soon as the train began to move, you couldn't hear anything on the phone. I called Bev a few more times. She was thrilled every time I talked to her. Before that time I would go 6 to 7 months without contacting anybody. They were so tickled that I had this phone. Now they could actually know that I was alive.

But when I got back to the Cities and went to Patty's house, my cell phone bill was waiting for me. I used Patty's address. The phone bill was $190. I didn't have the money, so I let the phones go. That was the end of my high stylin' it with a cell phone. It was fun while it lasted.

### Air conditioned comfort

I was hitch hiking from South Dakota down into Nebraska, and I got a series of short rides. Finally a guy picked me up. He worked for the railroad in Alliance. He drove me into town. He was an older, heavy set guy. He was very, very talkative. He was really curious about what I was doing in northwest Nebraska. He explained, "Well, there are trains here in Alliance, and they all go to Omaha. All of them are coal trains, but most have a "pusher unit." (The pusher unit was the locomotive at the rear of a freight train that was used to "push" the train.) I was thinking that maybe I could ride that pusher unit, because nobody would be in it.

I was broke. I didn't have a dime to my name. This guy gave me $10 and said, "Get yourself something to eat." He dropped me off on the west end of Alliance.

So, I walked into town, got myself something to drink. I was sitting on this bench, and this guy came walking up to me. He was kind of raggedy looking. He needed a haircut. He was maybe 5'9" , slim and had a shaggy beard. He looked like he had been out in the woods for a while. He approached me. "You're traveling, huh?"

"Yeah."

"Well, you know, I've been working out on the ranch for the past three months, and I haven't spent a dime. Want to have a beer?"

I said, "Yeah."

So, we went to have a beer, and then he handed me $100. He said, "Here. I don't need this." Then he said, "There's a restaurant over there. Let's go get something to eat."

Well, we drank a couple more beers and then went over there to eat. As we were sitting there, in walked his mom. She was an older lady with blue hair. She said to her son, "Now who is this?"

"Mother, this is my new friend. He's traveling. I thought I'd buy him something to eat." He never said a word about the $100 he had given me. We finished eating, and they left and I was sitting there with a $100 bill in my pocket. I was feeling pretty good. I could high style this for a while. So, I went into a liquor store and bought myself a half gallon of vodka, beer and some cigarettes.

I wasn't going to ride in a coal car, so I had to get in that rear unit—the "pusher." I had to get out of western Nebraska somehow. I saw the pusher there. The train was pointed east. I jumped up into this pusher. I sat in the captain's chair. The train got going, and I relaxed. Then in the middle of nowhere, the train stopped. We had gone about 10 or 15 miles, and now the train was stopped. I was wondering what was going on.

I was still sitting in the captain's chair drinking a beer. The train sat there and sat there.

All of a sudden, I saw this tall thin guy. He had a shaggy old mustache. He started climbing up into the unit—my unit.

Oh, shit. Now, I'm in trouble. We were out in the middle of nowhere, so it could only be the engineer or the conductor—either one. He started to climb into the unit, and I started to panic a little bit. What was I going to do?

He took a long look at me, and said, "I thought I had a hitch hiker back here. Where are you headed?"

I said, "East. Wherever this train is going."

"Well, we're going to Lincoln, then Omaha, and then Council Bluffs."

"Are you kicking me out?"

"Naw. I'm not going to kick you out, but don't touch a fucking thing. Here's your radio. Here the air conditioner, and if it does get cold, here is the heater. Don't touch anything else. And stay out of sight. Don't sit in that chair. Sit on the floor."

"OK, Boss."

"Oh, by the way. Here's a fridge for your beer." He got off the train and walked away. It was a smooth ride all the way to Lincoln. I was in air conditioned, high stylin' comfort.

## MY CODE OF HONOR

There is a code of honor when you are riding a freight train. It's unspoken. You just know that people will give you money. You don't have to steal from them. You shared what you had with your partners. If somebody new came into camp—as long as they announced themselves and looked decent, you invited them into your camp. If a guy was hungry, you gave him something to eat. If a guy was thirsty, you gave him something to drink. That was the code of honor. You also took turns flying a sign at a really good corner. You respected one another, because nobody else respected you.

If you start treating people decent, it would come back to you. I call it the "Wheel of Life." For example, one time I was in Yuma Arizona, and I got thrown in jail for assault. There was another tramp in jail with me. His name was "Country." We hit it off. We were both freight train riders. He was let out a few days before I was, and then he was transferred to prison. I was behind bars for 60 days before they let me out. I didn't know what happened to him, but when I walked out of the jail, there was a guy and gal sitting there. They looked at me, "Are you Fritz?"

"Yeah"

We're Dog and Cat. Country told us you were about to be released. Come with us."

I had no money. I didn't know a soul in town. I didn't know

them from Adam. It was a man and a woman. Their road names were "Dog" and "Cat", because they fought like dogs and cats.

It was just really, really great to get out of jail there with somebody waiting for me. They took me over to the Yuma camp. It was about 20 acres on the north outskirts of Yuma Arizona near the railroad tracks and the interstate highway. This land was set aside as a place where homeless people could set up a camp. They took me in to their camp for a few days to help me get on my feet.

Sometimes the code of honor required me to call the police. At one point I had a friend named Freeman. He was a sneak. Freeman was the home guard in Fargo. All of a sudden he was coming up with all this money. I said, "Freeman, where are you getting all this money?"

He took me to the Indian Center in Fargo—where people can get their mail. He went in and started sorting through these envelopes. He took this one and that one. Those envelopes were addressed to elderly homeless people. Freeman also found this gal who was willing to sign the check and say it was hers. He did this multiple times. One time he wound up with something like $1,400. I was thinking, "You know, it's going to take a couple of months to get this all straightened out. A social security check disappears, and it's not an easy thing to replace it. These people need that money. They can't take care of themselves the way Freeman and I could." I just decided that I could not ignore this. I didn't want Freeman doing it any more. So I went to the cops. All the cops in Fargo knew Freeman. It was so much a part of me that you don't snitch to the police. But I couldn't ignore Freeman hurting these elderly people. I assume the cops put an end to his stealing. I left Fargo, and I never saw Freeman again.

Here in St. Paul I really got involved with methamphetamines. For a time I was actually selling methamphetamines. I was selling to provide for my own habit. I got about $1,000 in debt to my dealer. He was starting to harass me about it. I thought, "I've got to do something. It's close to Christmas time. Now is an opportunity to bring in some serious money. So, I went up to Fargo. I was sleeping outside, and it was colder than Billy Hell. It was two days before Christmas. I made this sign. It read "Heading home to see my mom." Well, money started rolling in. I just stuffed it in my pocket. I counted my money when I went inside to warm up. "Oh, I've got a couple hundred dollars. I'm doing pretty good today."

I went back to my corner with that sign, and I got another pocketful of money. I did this three times, and the third time I went to warm up and count my money. I found three $100 bills all rolled up. Altogether I had $947. I began thinking. I knew my meth dealer. I knew his wife. I knew their kids. They lived in St. Paul. I'm pretty sure they didn't have anything. They weren't going to have much of a Christmas. So, I wired the money to the wife.

Then I phoned my meth dealer. I told him, "I'm not going to give you that $1,000 that I owe you. But I sent it to your wife."

"You can't be doing that. I need that money."

I said, "Yeah, your kids need Christmas too."

"I'm going to get you, Fritz. I'm going to get you."

"OK. But your wife and kids are going to have Christmas, aren't they."

"Fuck you, Fritz."

I hung up. I quit meth, and I never heard another word from the dealer.

### Random Acts of Kindness

I was in Salt Lake when I met James and Smoke. It was May, and we were in a camp in what was called The Killing Fields. It ran along the Rio Grande Railroad line. There had been numerous killings in that area. It was not a pleasant place.

James, Smoke and I were there together. Smoke was telling me about this old boy who would come into camp. "His name is David. He'll be here pretty soon."

Sure enough, here came this guy walking into camp. He was carrying a big box full of stuff. He shouted, "Yo to camp. Here I come."

The box had food in it: potatoes, lettuce, meat. You could make a stew out of what he brought. He asked, "What do you guys need? You need pots? Pans?"

"No, we got all that stuff."

"You need bedrolls?"'

"No, No."

Then he sat and talked with us a while. He was a recovering alcoholic. He had lived on the streets for years—drunk. Then he sobered up. He was in his 50's. I was in my 30's, so he seemed like an old timer to me.

He encouraged us not to drink. He said, "There's another way. Look at me. I was homeless. Now I'm bringing stuff into camp. I sobered up, and I met this wonderful woman. She pretty much takes care of me and lets me do what I want to do. This is what I choose to do."

I said, "You are a special man." I learned that he went to camps throughout Salt Lake. He was the local welfare.

One year I arrived in Sioux Falls in the spring time. I stayed there throughout the summer. On Thanksgiving day I figured there wouldn't be much traffic. I had enough money to buy myself a few beers. I'd take a day off from flying my sign. I took my beers and found a spot underneath a bridge. I was sitting there reading a book, drinking a beer.

I was thinking about Thanksgiving and my family. All of a sudden these two girls appeared—one had dark hair and the other very light hair. They looked like they might be 13 years old.

They were standing there with two plates, and I was thinking, "What the hell is this?" They had brought me a complete thanksgiving dinner—turkey, potatoes, dressing, gravy, the works.

"How did you know I was here?"

"Oh, we've known you have been here the last week or so."

"Thanks very much."

A couple hours later two more people appeared and they were bringing me Thanksgiving dinner. It was so special. People took time out of their lives to bring something to a homeless man.

One year I spent four or five months in Sioux Falls, South Dakota. Every day a dentist drove down my ramp. It happened to be my regular spot for flying a sign. He stopped and asked me what I wanted from McDonald's. Then he drove over to McDonald's and bought a meal and an extra sandwich, threw the change in the bag along with a McDonald's $10 gift card. Then he drove back and handed me the bag.

This dentist did this every day. I later learned that whenever there was someone standing at that corner, he would stop and ask what they wanted from McDonald's.

### Rescued by a Railroad Security guy

I was with two guys—one was from California and one was from Oklahoma. I'll call them Stan and Bernie. I suggested, "Let's go to Maine and have a lobster."

Stan said, "You're fucking nuts, Fritz."

But I picked up my gear and sat on the car waiting for the train to start heading east. After a few minutes Stan and Bernie appeared, "We'll go with you."

We changed trains in Minneapolis, and the next day we were 30 or 35 miles out of Chicago. I was sleeping with my feet hanging out at the end of a grainer. A railroad cop spotted my feet. He said, "You know, you guys can't be on this train."

"We're in the middle of nowhere."

"I don't care. You can't be on my train. If you don't leave, I'll have you thrown in jail."

"Fine." We got off the train and walked, it must have been five miles to Gurney, Illinois.

I was sick. We were out of booze. These two guys were hungry, so they went to a mission that they heard about. I couldn't eat. I was sitting there sick, and this guy walked up to me. He looked to be in his 40's. He was kind of ragged looking.

He looked at me and he said, "You want a drink?"

He offered me his half-filled fifth of vodka and he said, "Why don't you just take the bottle. I can get more."

I was just so grateful to this guy. He turned around and walked away.

Anyway the three of us finally came up with the money to take the regular commuter train into downtown Chicago. There we were in the middle of the third largest city in the country, and we didn't know where we were going. We didn't know where the railroad yards were.

The guy from California said, "Let's go to the library. I'll find a book that will tell us where the railroad yards are." He found the library, and when he found the book, we started looking at the railroad maps. We found out that Conrail would take us to New York.

We had the address and asked for the directions, and we were told to head south down State Street. Well, it started getting dark, and with every mile we covered, there were fewer and fewer white people. Soon the three of us were the only white people in a high crime area. We walked right through Cabrini Green. We finally got to the railroad yard. It was all fenced in. There was a tower right there. I knew a guard would see us. By now it was about 9 o'clock. A brown Dodge pulled up. A white guy got out of the car and walked over to the three of us, "What in the hell are you guys doing in this part of town?"

"Well, we're trying to get in that railroad yard."

"Well, I can't let you in there. I'm the head of railroad security here. I can't do it."

We just stood there. I was shaking my head.

"Let me see some ID's." I knew I didn't have a warrant in Illinois. Stan and Bernie said they didn't have any warrants in Illinois. He was gone for about ten minutes.

Then he came back and returned our ID's. Now it was really getting dark. He said, "Get the hell in my car."

I thought, "Oh, my God. I'm going to the Cook County Jail. That's the last place I wanted to spend the night."

He hauled us over to a little railroad yard. He said, "The fourth track over. There's a train. It's heading east in about ten minutes. Go find yourself a boxcar or something, and get the hell out of here. I don't want to find you dead tomorrow."

We walked about 50 yards into the railroad yard, and suddenly we had a gun pointed at us. The guy with the gun and a uniform was on the radio "I found these three fuckers."

We could hear the answer: "It's just three white guys."

"Yeah?"

"Well, get them the hell out of here."

We had been rescued from a dangerous environment by the railroad's head of security. We were relieved and grateful.

# 6

# Hard Times on the Road

## LONELY

I spent a couple days in Reading, California. Somebody told me I could get $100 in "GA" (general assistance) right away at the courthouse in Eureka. So I went over to Eureka. It was the mid 90's. I had been away from Betty and the boys since 1991.

It was Christmas Eve day. It was pretty nice weather. I was in northern California. It was in the 50's with a soft rain—typical weather for northern California, Oregon or Washington in December. I walked to the courthouse and found the welfare office. There I met a lady who was kind of stern and crabby. She was a heavy set lady, and she looked like she had just lost her best friend. She didn't seem real happy about giving me that $100 on Christmas Eve. I think she was just one of those crabby-by-nature people.

But I got my $100 in cash. Immediately I went to the liquor store. I got myself a half gallon of vodka. It cost $11. I always drank the bottom shelf vodka. I think it was Silver Wolf Vodka. There were so many of these bottom end vodkas—Silver Wolf, Grey Wolf, Kirkov. Depending upon where you were, there was always a wide variety of cheap vodkas. They sold for $10 or $12 for a half gallon bottle. They were always on the bottom shelf.

When you were high stylin', you went up a little bit.

I was feeling pretty low. Here it was—Christmas Eve, and I had nothing to do. The only reason I came to Eureka was to get the money. I thought about staying in Eureka and working the five days that were required for a payment of $500. I wasn't sure what I would do. I had no plans.

I walked toward the shore and the crabbing boats. There I found a cheap hotel. I could see the crabbing boats from the hotel. The hotel was run by an older couple. I had over $80 in my pocket, so I booked a single room for one night. It cost $32. It was a basic room with a TV, bed, chair and a desk and some sort of odd picture on the wall. It was a mountain scene.

I still had around $50 in my pocket. I was alright on cash. I sat down on the bed with that bottle in my hands. It was room temperature, but I didn't care. I was an alcoholic. Booze can be warm. I can drink out of a paper bag. I drank this vodka right out of the bottle. If I felt fancy, I would pour it out into a glass. But today I was not feeling fancy. I was feeling lonely.

I turned on the TV. It probably was something Christmasy. I opened the bottle. I took a long swallow, then another and another. I started getting drunk. I was feeling really, really lonely. I didn't matter to anybody. I had nothing. I had nowhere to go. Nobody really wanted me around because of the way I drank. If I died today, who would care? My family loved me but they didn't want me around. Mom and Bev were always there to answer the telephone and find out where I was at. They showed some concern that way. Several times a year, I called collect, and they always accepted it.

I held the phone in my hand, trying to decide what to do—wondering if I should call or not. I knew everyone would be at Bev's—Mom, Bill and his family, and of course, Bev and her family.

I was thinking about the times with my children and with

Betty. I didn't even have a photograph of my boys or my family back in McIntosh. But I thought of the Christmases a few years ago. We all went to Bev's place every Christmas Eve. One year Jeremy got a Nerf gun. It would shoot Nerf balls. We had a really good Nerf ball war that time. Josh, he got Legos. He loved his Legos. I was recalling the joy of watching these children open up their presents. I looked down, and the phone was still in my hands.

**My mother as she looked in the early 1990's.**

But I started feeling really sad. That little hotel room felt empty. I was wishing there was one other person that I could have there with me, so I wasn't alone. I had not been with anybody for 3 or 4 days. I had no plans—no plans to meet somebody.

My plan—kind of—was to go further down into California because there was a place down there in Fort Hood, California. They would gear you up with everything you needed for the winter—they would give you a backpack, a bedroll. I thought about going down there. But I had not made up my mind.

I put the phone down. I was still sitting on the bed, I pushed back and watched a little TV. Now I was really feeling sorry for myself. I was so alone. It was an emptiness that is so hard to explain. It is the loneliness and emptiness that goes through you when there is nobody around that cares.

I had Bev's and Mom's phone numbers memorized. I picked up the phone, and I dialed my sister's house. Bev answered the phone. I talked to her for about ten minutes. Then I talked to Mom for a few minutes. Finally, I talked to my brother for a little bit. When we got done, I hung up. Now I felt worse.

I felt worse because I wasn't there with them. They wanted me there so bad. They really did. Bev and Mom both cried and said, "Can't you come home, John? Can't you come home, John?" I felt so bad that I wanted to cry. Except I was a big tough guy, and I couldn't cry.

"No, Mom. I can't. There's nothing left for me in Minnesota." But yet, I kept going back to Minnesota. Minnesota was my saving grace. Every time I got so depressed and wanted to die, I headed back to Minnesota. I knew that I could attempt to sober up there.

I thought about it that day. Should I go back to Minnesota? Do I want to try one more time? Is it even worth it? I'd been in treatment a dozen times at least. I had not seen my boys in something like four years. Oh, I missed them. I missed those kids. I was wondering what they were doing on Christmas Eve now that they were in their teenage years. Where are they? Are they alright? I was completely alone. I was 1500 miles away from anybody I knew. I was feeling really alone and worthless.

### Cold

A week later I decided I would go back to Minnesota. I made it over to Spokane, Washington. It was early January. I was desperate. I had no place to go. So, I was thinking "home." It was time to go back to Minnesota. I had no idea what I would do when I got back to Minnesota. No idea. But I knew that there was somebody there who would tell me, "I love you." Somebody would actually show me that they cared. I was feeling really unlovable at this time. But I knew that as soon as they saw me, Mom and Bev would both hug me and cry.

I would be gone sometimes for a year or a year and a half at a time. I would let them know every three or four months where I was—that I was alive. But I would stay away for long periods of time. This time I probably had been gone for 13 or 14 months.

And I decided, "OK, I'm in Spokane. Let's gear up. Let's go."

I already had a pretty good sized bedroll. I had the sleeping bag and the quilt. I was about to cross that High Line. I knew it was winter time. Very few people do the High Line in the winter because it's so treacherous. It can drop down to 20 or 30 below with a blowing wind. You can get into snow storms. You don't know what you might get into.

The key was to prepare. We called it "gearing up." First, I found a 5" thick piece of foam rubber. It was just big enough for me to lie on. I found it behind a store—a mattress factory. I was looking for whatever I could find.

I knew that this foam pad would keep the cold out from under me. That's half your battle—keeping that cold from coming up underneath you. Then I needed a second quilt. I heard about this St. John's Catholic Church in Spokane. The word was that they would help you get geared up so you wouldn't freeze to death. They gave away blankets and clothes. You have these churches scattered around the country in different places. Word of mouth gets passed around from one homeless person to another. "You can get a bedroll at this church." So I walked over there. It was a big fancy old church. I went around to the back of it. A nun answered the door.

She invited me in and gave me a bag lunch. I told her that I was about to take a freight train across the High Line, and I needed an extra warm quilt. She didn't say anything at first. She searched through several big boxes and came up with the heaviest quilt she had. She handed it to me, looked me right in the eye and asked, "Are you sure you want to do that?" She seemed concerned.

I said, "Mam, I have to. I'm going to kill myself if I stay here."

So, now I had two heavy quilts plus my extreme cold weather bag. My bedroll was now three or four feet around. It was huge. I tied it with a rope and carried it over my shoulder. That's all I had. I wore all my clothes. I was wearing three pairs of jeans, a pair of long underwear, a couple of sweaters, a couple of flannel shirts, 3 or 4 pairs of socks. I had them all on my body. Now I was geared up.

I came up with the money for a half gallon. I think it was Silver Wolf vodka. I used to drink rubbing alcohol once in a while, and people would say, "How can you drink rubbing alcohol?"

I replied, "It really doesn't taste much worse than the vodka I drink." Now I was feeling pretty secure about going across country. I had a few dollars left in my pocket. I had a half gallon to drink and enough tobacco to get me a ways. I had enough to last me to Havre. Once I was on that train, it would take about 24 hours to get to Havre, Montana.

But I had never done this in the wintertime before. In fact, I had never ridden a freight train across the Highline. I had hitchhiked in the winter, but I never rode a freight train across the northern states. The old timers told me I was insane. They said, "It's really not worth it."

I said, "Well, I'm going home. I have to go home." I had to go home because I was ready to kill myself. I was ready to give up—the loneliness, feeling so worthless, so empty. I missed my kids. I missed my family. I was not going to see my kids but at least I would see the rest of my family. Somebody would give me a hug. I knew that I could sleep under a roof for a few days. I had to go.

At the Spokane railroad yard, I found a "twin stack" car. This is a flat car carrying two large containers with one stacked on top the other—hence "twin stacks." On those twin stacks you are pretty well protected from the wind. The platform is 2 ½' x 6'. The wind can come up from below. It is dangerous to try to stand up, because there is nothing to grab unto. If I stood up, I usually grabbed the ladder. If you do stand up, you are looking right at the knuckle (the coupling that connects the cars). That's why you pretty much lie down almost all the time.

I threw my bed roll up there. The weather in Spokane wasn't bad. It was 40 degrees out. But I knew that I was heading into some cold weather. When we pulled out of Spokane I thought,

"This isn't going to be so bad."

We headed into Idaho, and entered the mountains. The weather started dropping. It got colder. My fingers were getting cold. I tried to roll a cigarette, but my fingers were numb. I was shivering. I figured I better crawl inside my bedroll. So, I crawled in that bedroll in the middle of the day. Everything was covered except my face. Innside that sleeping bag I could warm up so I could roll cigarettes. My bottle was in there with me. I could take a nip. It wasn't really bad. But then we got into Montana.

Now we were up in the mountains, and I realized - this is going to be miserable. This is going to be cold. But I was committed. I was on the High Line. Once you are on that High Line, you are committed. Highway #2 is not a very good road to hitch hike. So, I was committed to this train going across country. There was snow everywhere. It was January, and days were short. I crawled up into that sleeping bag, and I drank. I drank myself to sleep. We stopped in Whitefish, and I woke up a little bit—just to stretch while we stopped for a crew change. Nobody bothers you in Whitefish. I got off the train and stretched a little bit. I took a pee.

The train started making air. That meant it was getting ready to take off. The brakes were air brakes. They were pumping up those brakes. You hear it. That's how you know a train is getting ready to leave. It is pumping up its air. We always listened for that, "It's making air. Let's get on."

I jumped back on. I still had about half of my vodka left. I was going to make it to Havre alright. The train took off, and it grew even colder. We were in northern Montana close to the Canadian border, and we hit open country. The wind blew. My face was feeling the exposed air. I was wearing a stocking cap as well as a hood over my head. I was lying down.

The real problem was the wind. The train was moving at about 50 miles per hour, and it was bitterly cold. It was too cold to try to hold a book. I just hid inside that sleeping bag. The only thing that I took off was my shoes. I hated sleeping in my shoes. I was

**A freight train drives through sub-zero cold.**

warm enough inside that sleeping bag. It was when I had to get out to pee or had to sit up and roll a cigarette, that I realized how bitterly cold it was. You could easily freeze your fingers in no time. You didn't dare touch the metal of the train cars. Anything made of metal was too cold. It would just go right through you.

When we arrived in Havre, I had to get off. I needed a break from that train. I went over to Walmart and flew a sign for a few days. I got enough money to get geared back up again—my booze and my cigarettes.

There was no break in the weather. It had to have been 10 below. I don't know what the temperature was, but it was cold. I would see puffs of steam coming out of my mouth when I breathed.

I got back on an eastbound train, another twin stack. I had made it halfway, and now I was pretty confident that I was going to get there. The bedroll was the key. I had 6 to 8 inches of quilt on top of me. I believed in layering up. Layers would keep me warmer. I drank myself to sleep.

The train pulled into Fargo. The closer I got to Minnesota the more I asked myself, is this really what I want to do? Do I want to go bother my family again? I began asking myself, "Do these people really want me to come? What am I going to do there? There is nothing there for me."

So, when I arrived in Fargo, I spent the night there. Actually, it was a railroad town a few miles east of Fargo—Dilworth, Minnesota. I slept outside, of course, and the temperature dropped down to 22 below. I got up the next morning. It was snowing and blowing. I had a few dollars in my pocket. So, I went into a bar and had a few drinks. It was nice and warm in the bar. I took some layers off.

Pretty soon people were buying me drinks. They saw my bedroll and asked, "Are you living outside?"

"Yeah. I just come across from Washington."

"You're one tough mother fucker, man. You better have a drink." So I got pretty drunk sitting in that bar. Meantime the weather outside was getting worse and worse. That bar was a railroad bar—right next to the big railroad yard. All the railroad yard workers drank there.

After a few hours of drinking, the weather was getting pretty bad, and I was getting pretty drunk. I was wondering what to do. Now I was out of money. My solution was to call my dad. He might come and get me. Sure enough. It was miserable weather out, and my dad came and got me. He drove down to Fargo in a snowstorm and picked me up.

### Jail

If you're homeless and riding freight trains, you're going to spend a fair amount of time in jail. I certainly did. I first became homeless when I was sixteen and didn't sober up and get a permanent roof over my head until I was 50. During those 34 years I spent four years in Minnesota state penitentiaries and another total of four years in jails in 16 different states—most of the time in Minnesota and North Dakota.

I quickly learned how to cope with going to jail. First, I didn't resist arrest. I never tried to run or fight. I never carried any weapons. I followed their directions Second, I didn't mouth off. I didn't talk smart. Third, I kept my sense of humor and usually joked with the jailors. These three lessons paid off. I was never abused by the police or the jailers. But that doesn't mean that I liked jail.

Jail was one of the downsides of my life style. I'll start with Havre, Montana. Havre is the halfway point between St. Paul and Spokane. The trains all stop in Havre; they change crews and check the trains. They refuel. In Havre, they have the railroad security men who walk the train. They make sure everything is alright. If you don't get out of that railroad yard right away, they will haul you to jail.

One time I woke up when the train stopped. It was a beautiful morning, and I didn't realize that I was in Havre. I started to jump off the train. But this railroad bull saw me. He called the city cops. They came and got me. They took me to this little tiny jail in Havre, Montana. It was a Friday afternoon. I had no idea. Were they going to keep me? Or were they going to let me go? Well, they kept me over the weekend.

Most jails don't want to keep you very long. It costs them something like $117 a day to keep a man in the local jail. The judge and the police force don't want to provide you with a temporary roof in their town. They want to get rid of you. But you never know. One time I was kept in jail for 60 days for throwing rocks at a guy. One thing is pretty certain—they don't tell you. They don't tell you anything.

That little jail in Havre had lousy food! The jails don't seem to feed very well anymore. You were given a hot dish. It might be some tomatoes, some hamburger and some macaroni. It tasted bland. For breakfast you got two boiled eggs and some hard toast. Every morning the same thing—two boiled eggs and some hard toast. At lunchtime you got a sandwich with meat so thin you could read the newspaper through it. I sat there for three days.

Finally, I was summoned to court. The judge fined me $150 and gave me three months to pay it. OK, I'm out.

A year later, I was coming through Havre, and the same exact thing happened. I jumped off the train, and there was the bull. I was locked up in the same little jail, and my cellmate says, "Weren't you here about a year ago?"

I said, "Yeah."

He said, "Well, I've been here for 14 months. I've been here all the time." He was in there for burglary or something like that.

Jail can be very confining. Let me describe some typical jail cells. You've got a two-man cell that is probably 6' x 8'. There are two bunk beds in there, and there is a stainless steel toilet and sink. There is no such thing as a toilet seat. There is a desk on the wall. You've got only 2 to 2 ½ feet of space where you can move around in the cell. At six feet wide, I could stand there and touch both walls.

You got two guys in there, and if you don't like your cellmate, what are you going to do? You've got to learn to get along with people. For some reason most jails are usually painted an ugly yellow. I heard that someone decided that yellow calms people down.

In the early years, I thought that cops had it in for me. But when I started getting thrown in jail wherever I went, I realized that the cops aren't calling ahead saying, "That Crazy Fritz is coming. You better get him in jail." I wound up in jail because I kept having behavioral problems. I recognized that.

I remember a little county jail in Arkansas. There were three of us locked up, and two guys taking care of the jail. We got peanut butter sandwiches and buttered noodles, and that was it. It was a miserable jail. There are jails all over the place. They are all the same. You get treated so poorly. Most jailers have no sense of humor. They are so tired of people coming in and giving them a hard time that they just immediately assume that you are going to give them trouble. But you don't have to. Often I went in joking with them. It usually defused the situation.

Sometimes it was very easy to get thrown in jail. That's what happened to me in Yuma, Arizona, in 1995 or 1996. It was the fall of the year. But it was still hot down in Yuma. It was a miserable day. I had $20 in my pocket. We were at the mission eating, and my buddy Fish got into this little spat with a guy in the mission over getting bumped.

My buddy Fish was an older white guy. He was from Texas—a carney (carnival) rat. He was rough looking—pock-marked face, 5'10", slim, in his 40's, blonde hair. Suddenly Fish took off chasing this skinny, older black guy. I decided I would go follow them to make sure that nothing happened between these two guys. It was an older black guy and an older white guy. I didn't want to see two old guys beat each other up. Suddenly this black guy stopped and swung this grocery bag at Fish. It was a bag full of canned goods. So, I picked up a rock, and I threw it at this guy to chase him off my buddy. I threw a couple more rocks. None of the rocks hit him. I was laughing about it. I was really not trying to hit him, but this guy climbed up over a fence, and his pants fell down. And now I was rolling with laughter and still trying to throw rocks at him. He got over to the other side of the fence, and I didn't think anything of it.

I thought, "OK. That's over and done." Fish and I went into a camp. We were drinking a half gallon of Bacardi rum. It was getting to be evening and cooling down. We had the campfire going. We had a full belly of food from the mission. We were sitting there. All of a sudden cops surrounded us. They arrested us for assault and armed robbery—for throwing a rock at this guy. I spent 60 days in jail in Yuma before they said they dropped the charges on me and let me go. It took them 60 days to decide what to do with me—while I was just sitting there. All I did was throw a rock at somebody.

I suppose the usual bad things about jail didn't bother me very much—being shamed by being arrested, being confined behind bars, the lack of privacy, being vulnerable to abuse by the jailers and others in the jail. Those things didn't bother me because I was used to far worse while homeless.

But three other things did bother me. First, I didn't like the tasteless food. I am a pretty good cook myself. I like good food. The jail food was depressing. Second, I enjoyed my freedom. Almost every morning I woke up and decided what I would do that day. In jail someone else was controlling me. I wasn't in control. I didn't know if I would be in that jail for another night or 60 more nights. It was the uncertainty and lack of control that was really hard on me. The third and worst thing for me was the withdrawal process and the DT's.

### DT's

I had been in treatment centers enough times to have a sense of what my blood alcohol level was at different times. It usually ranged from a point two (.2) to a point five ( .5). My highest level was .52 one time when I woke up strapped to a table with IV's in both arms in a detox center in Fargo. In Minnesota you can get arrested for a DWI if your blood alcohol measures at .08 or above. I considered myself pretty sober at point two which was two and a half times the legal limit. I learned that anything above point five can be fatal. My body could absorb a lot of alcohol.

I was a "low bottom" drunk. I'll explain that. A high bottom drunk still has a job and a car. A low bottom drunk is on the streets. A high bottom drunk probably drinks from a glass, and a low bottom drunk like me drinks out of a bottle wrapped in a paper bag. A high bottom drunk maintains a family and friends. A low bottom drunk has chased everybody away. A high bottom drunk doesn't drink in the morning. He has to go to work. A low bottom drunk is drinking pretty much 24/7. I was drinking a half gallon of hard liquor every day.

Any time I stopped drinking, I began to feel sick. My body would go through withdrawal from a steady dose of alcohol.

Within 36 hours of my last drink, I would be wracked with the DT's ("delirium tremens"). I have learned that only a few hard core drunks get the DT's. Casual drinkers and most heavy drinkers never experience this. But if you are regularly drinking a pint or more of hard liquor each day, you are vulnerable to the DT's. I was drinking four pints per day almost every day, so when I stopped drinking, my body really reacted.

This happened when I was locked up in jail for more than several days. It was the very worst part of jail. First, I would generally feel sick. Sometimes I would have the dry heaves. Then I started to shake. My stomach would hurt. Then my mind started to race. I couldn't slow it down. I couldn't sleep. I just got more and more agitated. Soon, I started to sweat. Then I starting hearing things and seeing things. I would hear someone calling me, "John! Whatcha doin'?" I would look all around and realize that nobody knew that my real name was John.

I remember being picked up in Fargo one time. I was shaky and sick. They wanted me to eat something, but when I tried to eat, I just puked. Falling asleep was worse than being awake because I had these terrible vivid, vivid dreams. I dreamt about a dead former friend. He was tearing the arms off my children and beating me with them. I knew it wasn't real, but it was so realistic. Next I saw and felt a giant tongue that kept licking me. Again, I knew it was not real, but it was so vivid. I was shaky and sweaty.

I heard voices shouting at me. But no one was there. Then some music started playing. It was rock and roll music, of course. Thank God it was rock and roll. But I had this stereo playing in my head. That stereo played for months. I was afraid it would be there forever.

In jail or in a detox center, they sometimes gave me Librium, and this greatly reduced the DT symptoms. But if I didn't have any Librium, I would start walking. I would be filled with anxiety, and I had to do something. The only thing I could do was walk. So, wherever I was, I would walk and walk and walk. I didn't want to fly a sign. I didn't want to talk to anybody. I just walked. Some days I would walk ten miles. As soon as I stopped, the thoughts came running back. There were voices asking me, "Why keep going? What is the purpose in all this?" I thought about killing myself.

The DT's were an obstacle to sobering up. I knew that if I tried to quit drinking, I was going to face the terrible DT's.

### Mental illness

I was diagnosed with mental illness in the early 1990's. I learned that I was bipolar. I was subject to big mood swings. When I was in a down mood, I was really down. I was prescribed medications to control the symptoms, and those pills worked pretty well. But when I felt good, I quit taking the pills, and the bipolar mood swings came right back.

### Close calls

It's dangerous to live on the streets. But most homeless people stay in their own hometown where it is not quite so dangerous. We called them the "home guard." Only a few homeless people ride freight trains, and that life style is even more dangerous. During my years on the road I had a number of very close calls—most of them could have killed me right then.

One of those close calls took place at a busy intersection in Fargo. It was 1996—a beautiful summer day. I had been drinking wine underneath an I-94 bridge in Fargo. I poured the last of the bottle into a coffee drinking cup with a lid and set off walking down 25th street toward the liquor store on the other side of 13th Avenue. The intersection of 25th Street and 13th Avenue was probably the busiest intersection in Fargo. But I had to get to the other side to reach the liquor store.

When I got to the intersection, the cars were lined up - stopped for a red traffic light. I was loaded down with my backpack, carrying my bedroll in one hand and in my other hand that cup filled with wine. I saw my chance to run across the street where the cars were stopped. I was about four or five cars back from the intersection. I jogged between the two lanes of stopped cars, but I was drunk and wasn't thinking about the third lane for left turns.

Smack. A small blue compact hit me. The car was probably doing about 20 miles an hour, and the impact sent me flying up in the air. I landed on the hood and the windshield. As I rolled off the hood, I was still holding my bedroll in one hand and my cup of wine in the other. I glanced at the car—the bumper was bent, the grill was smashed, the fender was crinkled and the windshield was smashed. I was now standing there about three feet from the driver. I looked at him. He was about 35 years old, staring at me.

I leaned forward toward him. His eyes were the size of saucers. I said, "Excuse me, sir." Then I turned around and continued my walk toward the liquor store. I had a small cut on my elbow, but I was quite pleased that I didn't spill any wine from that coffee cup.

Another time I was riding a freight train with two of my freight train buddies—Jaybird and Cutter. We were traveling together and had jumped on the train in Klammath Falls, Oregon - heading to California. For some reason we were riding on different cars. I remember feeling a jerk, a slam and a jerk. Suddenly we were stopped cold. We had been doing about 45 miles an hour. The train came to a stop. Just like that. I knew immediately that it was a train derailment.

My car somehow stayed upright on the track. The car behind me was upright but off the track. So was the car in front of me. It was a train wreck. All the other cars and the engine in front of me were all derailed and off the track. Several cars were piled up into a potato house. There were about 10 cars behind me, and they were all jumbled up. Our train load of lumber was scattered everywhere.

I jumped off the train to find my buddies. I found Jaybird a few cars ahead of us. He couldn't move at first, so I dragged him

**Our train derailed and crashed on September 18, 1991 outside Merrill, Oregon killing our buddy Cutter.**

away—afraid that something might explode. I looked around. Everything was a mess.

Jaybird came around, and he was OK. Cutter had to be close by. By this time the place was swarming with police and fire fighters. Nobody would go in and look for Cutter. They were afraid the cars were about to explode. My buddy was in there. I couldn't just leave him. So I went in.

I found Cutter. All I could see of him was his top half sitting on a big pile of dirt in the middle of the biggest puddle of blood I had ever seen in my life. He was dead. I don't know if he was cut in half or just buried in the debris. I don't know. I had never seen so much blood in my life.

It terrified me. I was scared to get back on a train. The TV reporters soon found Jaybird and me. We were eye witnesses to the train wreck. They asked us to do live interviews. Then the newspaper reporters wanted to interview us. We learned that we were five miles north of Merrill, Oregon. I was really shaken, but I wanted to act like a tough guy with my usual tough guy humor. So, when they asked us our reaction, I said, "Now that my train is wrecked, I'm worried about how I'm going to finish my trip to Portland." One person was killed in that train wreck and there was a lot of

H&N Photo by A.N. Valdez

**Remembering Tuesday's derailment are Jay Jacobson, left, and John Fritz who were riding the freight train.**

**Jaybird and I were briefly treated like celebrities when the local newspapers and television stations interviewed us as eye witnesses and gave us each $20 for our time.**

property damage. I have to admit I was really scared. I didn't ride a freight train again for some months. After the interview they gave us each $20. They also offered to send a copy of the paper to our friends and family if we supplied their names and addresses. My mom kept the newspaper to show me the next time I returned to McIntosh.

Winter—especially winter in Minnesota—is always a challenge for survival. Over the years I have never slept in missions. I always slept outside- even during the winter. If I had a good bedroll, I didn't worry about freezing to death during the night. But I had a close call one winter night in Fargo. I was drinking pretty heavy that night. It was about 10 degrees above zero, and I must have passed out. I was lying there without a blanket. I didn't have any shoes on. Fortunately, I woke up. My feet were very cold. I thought they were frozen. I was in Fargo that night, and I went to a "wet shelter." (There are only a few wet shelters in the country. They accept people who have been drinking.) I thought maybe my feet were gone. They hurt a lot, but I didn't lose my feet. I've still got them. My feet bothered me for two or three years. Whenever it grew cold, my feet would begin to burn.

One night a bunch of us were partying. You never knew what was going to happen when you started partying with a bunch of homeless men. Chances are they were all drunks and most of them had some kind of mental illness. There was Brian (who was an Indian from northern Minnesota), Dan and I and several others. The next thing you knew, Brian was attacking me. He had his knife out. Brian was 5'10" and maybe 180 pounds. There was absolutely no reason that I could figure out. But he was coming after me with a knife. I was jumping out of the way and dancing around.

He thought he was going to get me with that knife. But I knocked him over and jumped on top of him. I grabbed the knife, and I just threw it as far as I could throw. Then I let him up and said, "Have you had enough?" He just walked away. I never found out what happened to the knife, and I never saw Brian again.

Knives are dangerous. Pistols are worse. I was in Las Vegas in June one year. It was miserably hot out. The sun was blazing down on us 18 hours a day. It was 100, 110 every day. We used to set up camp in the parking garage of the El Rancho hotel and casino. The gambling commission in Nevada had shut it down. There were 60 or 70 homeless men living in this parking garage. There were five floors and people scattered around each floor.

It would be so hot at night time, that you wanted to sleep up on the roof so you would get a little wind, but if you stayed on the roof, the sun would come up at 5 o'clock in the morning and start cooking you. So, you either suffered at night time or suffered in the morning.

Right across the street was an empty lot—next to Circus Circus. A bunch of us hung out there—Rob, Dan, some other guys and I. Dan was a short guy—about 5'6", stocky. He liked to talk. He was a loudmouth. He was always boisterous—always thinking he could do this and he could do that. He was a character. According to him, he could do anything. He could remodel houses; he could build cars. Most of us knew that he was just full of shit. But Dan and I got to be pretty good friends. We pan handled together. We drank together. We slept up in the same part of the parking garage.

On the Vegas strip I met a girl named Sunny. She handed out flyers for a bar. She was really, really cute—a little blonde girl. She might have been 5'2" and 125 pounds. She was a beautiful young lady. We got talking, and she told me, "John, if you'd ever clean up, I would go out on a date with you."

She and I got to liking each other. She invited me home one time with her roommate's permission. I went over there to clean up. Sunny and her girlfriend were regular people. They had a house. They had furniture. They had curtains on their windows. It was something I wasn't used to. There was food in the fridge. They cooked for me. They let me shower up. I drank their beer, smoked their pot. Then they took me back down to the Strip. They did this four or five times. They were just being good people to me.

One day Dan was with me, and they asked me if I wanted to go and get cleaned up. I said, "Sure, Sunny, let's go."

Dan said, "Well, can I go too?"

I said, "Why not?" I had been hanging out with him for a couple of weeks and I thought I could trust him.

Well, we got over to Sunny and Debbie's place. They had a couple cases of beer. Both Dan and I showered up. They grilled out for us. Actually grilling out was not a big deal for me because I cooked outside anyway. But it was nice to have somebody treat me like I was a regular human being. It had been a while since anybody had acted like I actually mattered. Sunny made me feel like she did care, like I mattered to somebody.

They were driving us back to the strip. I was sitting in the back seat with Sunny, and mostly I was thinking about having sex with her. I was focused on Sunny. Debbie was driving and Dan was sitting next to her. I guess he opened the glove compartment and saw a loaded pistol. He snatched it and jumped out of the car at the next stop sign.

Debbie shouted, "He's got my gun." I jumped out of the car and chased after him. I caught up with him. I grabbed him and spun him around. He pointed the gun right at my face. Without thinking I snatched that gun out of his hand and started pistol whipping him. I shouted at him, "If you point a gun at me, you better mean to use it." He was all bloodied up. He had a cut in his head and a bloody nose. He took off running. I gave the pistol back to Debbie. There were tourists standing all around.

As soon as it was over, the adrenaline started coming down. I realized that I could have been shot very easily. I never thought about it at the time, but now I was thinking about it. I started to shake—literally. Debbie and Sunny were thanking me, but my mind was elsewhere. "What are you doing? Are you trying to kill yourself? The man could have shot you. If he had his finger on the trigger when you grabbed the gun, the pistol would have fired."

I had another close call with death one morning in Fargo. I was in and out of Fargo all the time because it was close to home. It was as close to home as I really had in those days. I was with Dougie Brown. It was about 11 o'clock on a beautiful summer morning. We were sitting there, pretty drunk already. Dougie was a Native American. He was a cousin of my old friend Freeman Brown. Dougie was kind of a thin guy. He was also kind of slow in the head. Dougie and I were sitting there sharing a quart of whiskey. We had smoked up the last of our cigarettes. We saw some guys down the track about 100 yards from us. They had a camp there in the shade of some nice trees.

Dougie decided that he was going to walk down to this other camp, and see if he could bum a cigarette. He was gone for maybe ten minutes. When he came back, he was huffing and puffing.

"Those assholes. They wouldn't give me a cigarette. They threatened to beat me up." There were three of them.

I said, "I'll go get us a cigarette." So Dougie followed me back to their camp. I was wearing a brand new Jeans jacket. When you are on the street and you have something like this brand new jacket, you are really proud of it.

When we got to their camp, there were these three guys, drinking and smoking cigarettes, and I said, "Hey, give me a cigarette."

This guy said, "No."

"Aw, come on. Gimme a cigarette."

"No."

This guy was short and skinny with a scruffy beard. We'll call him Larry. So, I bumped him with my chest. "Come on. Gimme a cigarette."

He pulled out this pop bottle full of gasoline, and he said, "I'll squirt you with this and light you on fire."

I bumped him again. "Gimme a cigarette."

He squirted gas at me. But still I never dreamed that the guy would light me on fire.

I bumped him once more, and he flicked his Bic cigarette lighter and lit me on fire.

Dougie grabbed my jeans jacket and jerked, and that brand new Jeans jacket came off in two pieces. It lay there and smoldered. I wasn't hurt. I said, "OK. Now will you give us a cigarette?"

"Sure. Sure. Let's have a drink too." I wound up getting drunk with the guy.

I will describe one more close call. This was in a small town down in Mississippi with Linda. We were up underneath a bridge. Linda and I were having a good old time living under this bridge—staying drunk. There was a grocery store where you could buy beer or whiskey or whatever you wanted, right down the road. We kind of had it made. We had money. We had booze. We had cigarettes and a dry place to live. We thought we might stay there for a few days.

That was until these three kids stopped to take a pee under the bridge, and I yelled at them. They were three white kids—early 20's. They were red neck kids. When I yelled at them, it scared the shit out of them. They took off. They were surprised. They hadn't seen us.

An hour or so later, they came back. One guy had a beer bottle in his hand. He seemed to be the leader. I didn't notice if the other two had anything. I stood up and walked toward them. I was focused on the lead one. I was thinking, "This is the one that I got to worry about first."

He had this beer bottle. He was holding the neck of the bottle like a club. So I reached back to grab a stick lying by my feet, and one of the other guys shouted "Don't." I was thinking that maybe he had a pistol.

OK. OK. Now what am I going to do. We're in a shit situation here. It was still daylight out, but these kids didn't give a shit. We were all up underneath this bridge where no one could see or hear us. They could have really fucked me up real bad. So the lead guy stepped forward and swung and hit me on the head with that bottle.

I just stood there and looked at him. I didn't flinch. It hurt. Oh, God, it hurt. It does hurt to get hit in the head with a bottle. Getting hit with a beer bottle is not quite as painful as getting hit with a wine bottle, but it hurts a lot. I joke about it, but it does hurt. Blood started coming down my face, but I had to stand here. I had to be a man—do what I could do.

I think maybe it freaked them out. I hadn't flinched. I just stood there—waiting for them. The three of them walked away. Maybe they were just messing with us, and maybe they really meant to do something. I didn't really think about the danger that we were in—until afterwards. Then the adrenaline started flowing. I could have gotten beat up here—really, really bad. Something terrible could have happened to Linda.

Linda and I packed up the camp and moved. In the midst of

something like that, I didn't have a whole lot of feeling. I reacted to what was happening around me. And then, after the fact, the fear set in. The terror set in.

### ASHAMED

It was the fall of the year. Things were starting to get brown. It was still nice weather out—in the 70's. I had come from Salt Lake where I was with James and Smoke. I split with them in Idaho and came over into Montana. Now I was by myself in Havre, Montana. I wasn't feeling really good about myself anyway. I had not talked to my family. I was feeling like I should be doing something. I should be working. I should be accomplishing something, buying cars, buying homes. But I was not doing any of this. I was really ashamed of myself.

So, I was out there in Havre, Montana flying a sign. I was ashamed of myself for standing there with a sign. Here I was—begging again. On the sign I had written: "Homeless. Traveling. Need help." It was all true, but still I was ashamed of myself for standing there. People look at you, and you just kind of crawl inside yourself because they think, "What a bum! Look at that guy. He's worthless."

Sometimes people would roll down their window and shout, "Get a job." It hurt. The shame built. There is a difference between guilt and shame. You have guilt when you are sorry for something you did. It's shame when you feel bad for who you are.

So, I was standing there at the exit of the Walmart parking lot, flying a sign, feeling really shitty about who I was—how I could have done so much more with my life. I was standing there with that pain gripping me. Suddenly there was this guy coming up to me. He had a black beard, was wearing a homemade blue shirt and black pants and a black flat top hat. He was in his late 30's—about my age. He was followed by a pack of kids. The oldest was about 16 and the youngest about four. It looked like they were all wearing homemade clothes. He walked up to me and said, "Hello, sir. How are ya?" He had a German accent. I figured he was from the local Hutterite community.

I looked at him, and I said, "I guess I'm alright. But I'm not sir. I'm John."

He continued, "Maybe life is bad right now, but you know, things can get better." This guy was trying to cheer me up.

He said, "Well, here's a few dollars for you." He held out a twenty dollar bill.

He was trying to make me feel better, but with every word I was feeling worse. I said, "Man, I don't need your money. Give it to those kids. I've got a few dollars in my pocket."

"No. No, sir. You take this money. You need it a lot worse than we do." He was calling me "sir" again. Calling me "sir" somehow made me feel worse. I should be calling him "Sir." He's the one who was actually doing something with his life. I was just standing there, begging for money again. Everywhere I went, all I did was stand around begging money. I didn't know anything else.

I took the money. I took that money that he could have spent on his kids, and that shamed me even more. He gave me money thinking that I would go and buy myself some food. I took that money, bought some booze and walked around behind the Walmart and drank it up. Then I got up the next day and did the very same thing. I felt this guilt from taking stuff from people who needed it worse than I did. These people were trying to help me, and all I wanted to do was hide and drink—hide behind the store, sit by myself and drink.

# 7

# Prison

## I assault a man

My life took a major turn in the fall of 2000. It all started with the death of my uncle Bob Fritz. He was my father's younger brother. At the time of his death, Uncle Bob was estranged from his only child. He made a fair amount of money during his life as a surveyor working in oil fields from Alaska to the Middle East. When he died he had an estate worth almost $500,000. To everyone's surprise he left it in equal parts to two of my brothers—Bob and Bruce. Each of them received over $200,000. Almost everyone in the larger family was mad. I didn't care. But most of my family was upset. I think this is exactly what Uncle Bob wanted. I think he wanted to stir up trouble. He did.

I was always close to Bruce, and Bruce was drinking really, really heavy at the time. He was also an easy touch for people who wanted something from him. He was trying to build himself a house on 40 acres just outside McIntosh. We had planted a nice tree line there when we were kids. He had a few horses, and now Bruce was building himself a house on the land.

People were persuading Bruce to lend them money and buy this and do that, and he was down to $120,000. He was drunk all the time and giving away money. I thought, "I can't have this going on." So I offered to come up to McIntosh, help him finish his house and chase away the free loaders. One of the free loaders was a guy named John Sander. He was married to one of my nieces, but he was bad news. John Sander was a liar and a thief. He never worked. His wife (my niece) worked and supported the family. Then he abused her. He beat her up. She never pressed charges. Bruce was paying John to help him build his house. When I came to help out on the house, he was there.

John was in his 30's—scruffy looking, about 5'10" and 165 pounds with long hair. Although Bruce was paying John to help him build his house, I sensed that John was ripping off Bruce. I didn't like him beating up my niece either. Bruce had lost canoes, generators and other stuff at the building site. Stuff was disappearing. Although I had no proof, I thought John Sander was the main culprit in ripping off Bruce. I wanted to put an end to it.

So one night I confronted him. I punched him once, and he ran. We caught him and took him to Bruce's place which was under construction. I thought I would slap him around a little and get him to confess what he had stolen and name his friends who had stolen things from Bruce.

I was wiring the house at the time, and I used some spare "twelve two" electrical wire to tie him to a wooden chair. Now I would get to the bottom of how John had cheated my brother Bruce. I hit him a couple of times. I was drunk myself, and I didn't really have much idea of what I was doing. At first he denied everything. Then he fell over backwards and broke the chair. I suddenly went into a rage. I wanted him to confess. I got the brilliant idea to torture him a little with some electrical wire. I stripped the ends of some wire and plugged it into an electrical outlet and touched him with those two exposed ends. Nothing happened. Then Bruce joined me and poured a little beer on his bare chest. I touched him briefly again, and this time he shook violently. I removed the wire, held it in my hand and told him to start talking. He did. He started confessing to what he had stolen and what others had taken. I threatened to touch him again, and he started shouting that this guy did this and that guy took that.

Then I realized what I was doing. For some reason I dug up a revolver I had stored at the house. It was a big 30/30, and I threatened him, "Well, I guess I can't let you go now." I fired a shot through the roof.

Now he was really scared. He thought he was going to die. He said, "Tell my wife I love her." That was my niece he was talking about. I knew he had slapped her around and hit her, and she never pressed charges. I was really angry.

I said, "I can't let you go."

He screamed, "I won't tell anybody." I thought my 30/30 was making big holes in the house, and I switched to a small .22 and shot over his head. My brother Bruce was watching, and he was laughing like a schoolgirl. John Sander was finally getting what he deserved. I shot over his head again, and he screamed, "I won't tell anybody."

Eventually I untied him. He could have left right away, but he stayed with us. We all stretched out on the floor and slept through the night. He left in the morning, and Bruce and I returned to our work. We installed the furnace the next morning. Then we drove to nearby Fosston and got some more booze. We were back at the house, drinking and listening to the radio. We were having a good time.

### The local police arrest Bruce and me

That night around 9 o'clock, it was dark and quiet when suddenly the doors of the house were kicked in, and a dozen cops surrounded us with their guns drawn. I was pressed face down on the floor and cuffed.

They threw Bruce and me in different police cars and drove us to Crookston to the county jail. I was sitting in the back seat, and

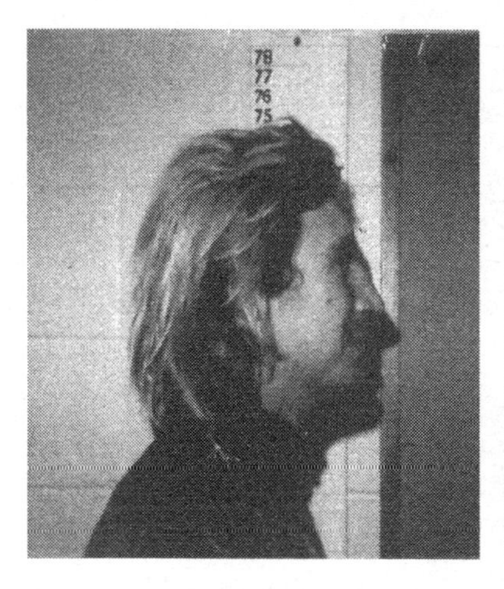

finally I asked, "What in the hell is going on here?"

The lead cop said, "Well, you're charged with kidnapping and attempted murder."

That annoyed me and hurt my pride, so I said, "If I attempted to murder somebody, they would be dead." We arrived in Crookston at the Polk County jail. We were locked up in adjoining cells—each about 8 feet by 12 feet in size.

### The sentence

I didn't have any money, so I had nothing but a public defender. But Bruce had money, and he hired a lawyer. Bruce's lawyer told us that we were charged with kidnapping and attempted murder, and their first offer was 30 years in jail for each of us. That really scared me. I was 41 at the time. I would be 70 by the time I got out.

Bruce and I started to talk. What are we going to do? I immediately got the DT's as I started to withdraw from the alcohol in my system. It started about eight hours after my last drink. I sweated. I shook. I felt nauseous. A lot of people throw up when they go through withdrawal but I didn't. It lasted about three days. I walked. There was an area about 90 feet long, and I walked and walked and walked. I knew that Librium would reduce my suffering, but they just let me suffer.

Bruce and I were also dying for a cigarette. We solved that problem. We were put in neighboring cells, and we carefully dug a hole in the wall right by the window to the outside. Bruce hired a kid to come and sell us cigarettes. The going rate for cigarettes was $5 in that jail, but Bruce paid this kid $100 to poke a carton of cigarettes one by one through this hole. We also had cigarettes mailed to us using a fictitious lawyer.

We settled down to figure out how to negotiate our sentence. Bruce kept paying his lawyer, and we turned down their first offer of 30 years. In the Polk County jail they evaluated most inmates. Some were sent down to St. Peter for further mental evaluation. They never evaluated Bruce and me. I guess they thought we were sane.

There were about 50 inmates in a space designed for 29. A few of them thought they were tough. One day I was sweeping the floor, and this kid came up and tried to grab the broom from me. He said, "I need to sweep out my cell."

I said, "No. I'm sweeping. Just leave me alone."

Then he grabbed the broom. That got me mad. I pushed him. He pushed back. Next thing you know, I pushed him back against the wall and wrapped the metal handle of the broom right around his neck. Then I hit him a few times. He shouted "No. No. No. No."

Suddenly jailers appeared. We both said, "We're OK." It was the only trouble I had in 14 months at the Polk County Jail.

When I was at the Polk County jail my brother Bob came to visit us one time. He had become a Christian by then, and he tried to preach at me. I told him, "I don't want it." I got up and walked out. My whole family—my mom, my sister Bev and the rest—they were pretty mad at me. Bruce had several visits, but I didn't. I really didn't want visitors because this dragged me out into the real world.

In the meantime Bruce's lawyer was negotiating on our behalf. He got the charge reduced to first degree assault. Then he reported that he could get the charges reduced to second degree assault with a sentence of 58 months for me and 81 months for Bruce. Bruce already had a prison record for felonies, so he would get a longer sentence. I still wanted to fight, but Bruce accepted the deal. It was called an Alford Plea. I kept saying that I wanted to fight this up until the day of the trial. We could call character witnesses. John was a well known liar and thief. Finally it was judgment day in the courtroom, and they were selecting a jury. Bruce accepted the 81 months, and Bruce's lawyer came over to me.

"Look, John, if you don't take this, they are going to throw the book at you. They are going to bring back the charge of attempted murder. I will represent you, but I don't think we can win. They are going to find you guilty, and then they are going to hit you hard. You better take the 58-month plea." He scared me. I decided to take it.

The normal sentence for what we did would have been 21 months but they increased it almost threefold because of the heinousness of the crime—the torture. It was February of 2002, and we had been in the Polk County jail for 14 months. Now we were both going to prison for some hard time. (John Sander had reported both of us, and I suppose he was happy that we were sentenced to hard time. Bruce and I both would serve our time and get on with our lives. John was arrested later for burglary, and he is in prison himself in 2016 as I write this story.)

I was scared. I had never been to prison. Bruce had been in prison. He kept telling me it was no big deal. Just stand up for yourself. But I was terrified. I was 41 years old. I was thinking I was pretty old to start going to prison. Most of these kids who go to prison are in their 20's. I was a little worried. I was a lot worried.

### CASTLE GRAY SKULL

They picked us up at the Polk County Jail and hauled us over to St. Cloud. The deputy sheriff in Crookston drove us, and when he

**St. Cloud State Penitentiary and its famous granite wall**

took us out of jail, the first thing he did was buy us a pack of cigarettes. He let us smoke all the way down to St. Cloud. I smoked so many cigarettes so fast that I started getting sick from the nicotine. We got to St. Cloud. They called it Castle Gray Skull. It is a big stone building with a huge wall around it. It's on highway 10 just the other side of St. Cloud. They say that the prison wall is the second longest continuous wall in the world—second only to the Great Wall of China. I was wearing street clothes. They brought us through that gate, and the gate shut behind us. I remember that gate shutting on me.

Everybody that comes into the Minnesota state penitentiary system starts at St. Cloud. When you walk in that door, and you hear it "cling" shut on you, it just sends a chill through your body. Then there was a bunch of paperwork. They took us over to where they dressed us. Bruce and I got out of civilian clothes and into penitentiary clothes. You have plastic banded pants. You don't have a belt because a belt is dangerous. You have blue work shirts and really cheap tennis shoes. They are so thin that when you walk you can feel the rocks right through the soles. The rocks poke you in the foot.

They put Bruce and me in adjoining cells. The cells were six feet by 12 feet. You could reach across and touch both walls. They locked us down. It was damp and muggy, and it stunk. The worst part was the noise, the noise of hundreds of guys yelling and shouting. It was so noisy, I couldn't think.

The first days we were locked up in our cells while we were tested for different diseases. Meals were served to us through the book pass—an opening about 6" by 15" where they pass you your meals or a book or anything. I sat in my cell with nothing to do. A guy came around with books, and I grabbed a book. You couldn't get a TV until you had been there 30 days. All I could do was sit there, read and think.

The food was good. There were roast beef sandwiches with nice slices of beef. There was no pork of any kind because of the Muslims. We had turkey bacon, turkey sausage—everything was turkey. You ate real good, but you had to eat fast. You never knew how long you had. It might be 15 minutes. It might be less. It all depended on your correctional officer as they called them—how long he felt like sitting in the chow hall waiting for you. I learned to eat fast.

Bruce and I checked on the black market price for cigarettes. We learned the going rate in St. Cloud was $10 per cigarette. The guards were bringing them in for $5 a cigarette, but then they had a markup. Bruce had a can of rolling tobacco smuggled in by a guard. It cost him $1,000, but he rolled cigarettes and sold them and made his money back.

Then they brought us to the office and started evaluating us. If you got really high points, you were sent to Oak Park. That was for the highest class (worst) offenders. The next worst stayed in St. Cloud or went to Stillwater or Rush City. Then there are the medium security prisons—Lino Lakes, Moose Lake and Faribault. I only spent 27 days in St. Cloud before they told me I was being transferred.

At St. Cloud I had almost no communication with the outside world—only a couple letters from my mom. Mom and the rest of the family were fed up with Bruce and me—our behavior and going in and out of jail. We had humiliated the family.

### To the "gladiator school"

I packed up my stuff, but I didn't know where I was going. They don't tell you until you are on the way. "You're going to Rush City."

Rush City was a brand new prison. It was high tech with all the latest equipment. It was also the "gladiator school." Tough young guys from the Cities were sent here—Hispanics and Indians, Whites and Blacks—mostly Blacks. Many were gang members. There was the Aryan Brothers, the PMB, the GD's and so on. The typical guy was 18 to 30 and trying to prove how tough he was. There were over 1,000 men at Rush City. That's a lot of testosterone. There was a lot of hostility. You could feel it.

As soon as I arrived, I was confronted by a group of Indians. They handed me a list. I said, "Oh you're going to buy me some stuff?" I knew they were trying to strong arm me, intimidate me into giving them stuff. I said, "What the hell, you think I'm going to do—give you something?"

The leader paused, and then he said, "Well, let's see your papers to see what you are in for."

I threw my papers toward him. He looked at the papers and said, "You're a real criminal." I gained respect for taking care of my family—watching out for them. I had some status. I was a respected criminal. I was watching over my niece to make sure her husband was not beating her up. I was considered one of the higher ranking prisoners. There is a very clear pecking order in prison. At the top are the lifers—people in for murder. Next come people like me—who assaulted people on behalf of their family. Then came the burglars and swindlers and so on. At the bottom were those charged with sex crimes. The child molesters were the very worst. We called them "Cho Mo's." They were despised and were vulnerable to getting raped or beaten.

There were gangs in prison, and there was a lot of extortion. I stood just over six feet tall and weighed about 235 pounds. I had been in plenty of fights. I seldom lost. I stayed away from trouble, but if trouble was in my face, I never backed down. I never had any real trouble. They left me alone.

You had to be careful at Rush City—not just with other inmates but with the guards. The word was that when Rush City opened, they staffed it with the misfit jailers from around the state. Some of them were mean. You had to be careful. The guards could also be very petty.

For instance, one morning, I said "Hi" to a female lieutenant guard.

She turned on me and snarled, "What did you say to me?"

I told her that I said hi.

"Well, that's not what it sounded like." It was stuff like that. You didn't dare talk to them. They would throw you into the hole.

Another time a female guard was following me as I walked up the stairs, and she said, "Fritz, you've got a really nice ass." This was a correctional officer saying this. I didn't know what to say. I decided to be real careful. I didn't want to get caught in the same room with her. She could claim anything, and it would be her word against mine.

The typical punishment in prison was "the hole." You got sent there for 21 days, and you were in a separate area of the prison and confined to your cell. They passed you three meals a day through the "book pass" and you just sat there. I spent 42 days in the hole in my first two months at Rush City before I figured out how to avoid it.

### Cursillo weekend and studying the Bible

Once I settled in to the routine at Rush City, some lifers told me about the Cursillo Weekend that was coming up. It was a group of Christians from various churches that came to Rush City for a long weekend of study, singing and fellowship. Prisoners could apply to participate. These guys told me it was a good deal. You got out of your cell, the people were very nice. It was a good experience. So, I signed up.

I had a very good experience. For one thing, these church people treated me like a real human being. They called me, "John." That may not sound like a big deal, but in prison I was a number. I was 208573. That was the number on my badge. If I went to the store to buy something, I gave them my number. They didn't care what my name was. But these people were kind. We studied. They had some really good upbeat Christian music. I liked it. They sat down right beside us and ate with us. I got inspired. I said, "Maybe there is something to this Christianity." I started reading the Bible. In fact I got several different versions of the Bible. I was reading the Bible real heavy. I read it from cover to cover—five times. I thought maybe Christianity could turn my life around for when I was released from prison. I started going to the worship services at the prison. That was a positive experience at Rush City, but I also had a very negative experience.

### A miserable visit and devastating letter

I got a letter from my dad saying that he, Eva (his second wife) and my son Joshua were coming to visit me, and he gave me the date. I was very apprehensive. I had been locked up for about 2 ½ years, and I had only one visit, and that was almost two years ago. In his letter my dad didn't say why he wanted to see me, and he didn't say what he wanted to talk about. He just said that he was going to visit me. First of all, I had apprehension because I really didn't want visits to start with. I didn't want to be dragged into the outside world. This was my life right now. I was in prison. I didn't need to deal with problems out in the world. Second, I was very apprehensive about the visit because my dad - well, it's always all about him. He didn't really care about me. Third, I didn't know where Josh was going to be—where his mindset was at. I had not seen him in over 10 years. Now he would be seeing me in prison. So, right off the bat, I was fearful.

I learned that Josh had come to stay with my dad for the summer. I heard about that. That was the first time I had heard where Joshua was in over 10 years. I had not seen Josh since 1991 when he was 8 years old. Now this was 2003. So, it was 12 years since the last time I saw him. He wasn't a little boy anymore. He was 20 years old at this point.

I didn't know how he was going to react. When they came into the prison, it started off that my dad couldn't get in because he was wearing bib overalls. Those overalls have metal on them, so he had to find something else that he could wear. They were late getting there to start with. That made me even more apprehensive. I was sitting there—waiting, waiting, waiting. I started thinking, "Why are they coming to see me?"

To get to the visiting area, I had to go through a strip search. You get out of your clothes, and they tell you to bend over and spread your cheeks and all that. Every prisoner who gets a visitor has to go through that. Then when you are coming back out of the visiting room, they strip search you again. That strip searching is very humiliating. You bend over, spread your cheeks, lift your nuts…it is just part of the degradation of being in prison. The prisoners have the right to say, "No. I don't want to see this visitor." I thought about doing that—saying, "I don't want to deal with this right now."

Anyway, I walked into the visiting room. It was a big, open room. The rows of chairs were set up four feet apart. The prisoners sit four feet away from their visitors. They are not allowed to touch. You are allowed one hug at the beginning as they come in and one hug when they leave. There are other groups scattered around the room with other prisoners and their visitors.

At that time, I was in one of the worst spots of my life. I was sitting in the penitentiary. Josh had been fed stories about how rotten and no good I was. I was worried. When they arrived in the visiting room, we didn't hug at all. I took a seat about four feet away from them. I looked at Josh. I recognized him immediately. Josh wouldn't say a word. My dad chattered and chattered and so did his wife Eva. They told me all about what was going on in their lives. Josh sat there and wouldn't say a word. He didn't ask me a thing about me. For that matter, my father didn't ask me anything about myself or my experience in prison. For my dad, it was all about him.

I tried to draw Josh out. As my dad and his wife were talking, I kept glancing over at Josh, trying to read his mind. His facial expression was really flat. He didn't seem to be happy or sad. It was like I didn't matter to him. When I tried to draw out Josh, he said almost nothing. He had one word answers like "Yeah" and "No."

Nobody smiled except Eva. She smiled and chattered. The more I tried to draw out Josh, the sadder I became. It was awkward. Dad and Eva wanted to leave and let Josh and me talk, but that terrified me. How was I going to get this boy to talk to me? So, I said, "No. No. You might as well stay." They stayed for about 45 minutes altogether. Josh said very little. The only thing I remember is that he told me that Jeremy was in a boot camp for juveniles. He got busted for guns or drugs or something. Rather than sending him to a real prison, they sent him to this boot camp for juveniles. Visiting time was two hours, but they were getting ready to go.

Finally, I turned to Josh and said, "Josh, please write to me. Let me know what's going on with you." He grunted OK.

A few days later I got a letter. It was from Josh. I opened the letter and started to read. The letter was addressed to "John." He didn't call me "Dad." It read, "John, you're a piece of shit. You are just what my mother always said you are. You are no good. I never want to see you again. I'm sad that I even went to see you this time."

This tore my heart out. I was so close to my children when they were young. Now all of a sudden I was being told I was good for nothing, and they don't want to see me. It devastated me. At that point I decided I would refuse all future visitors. I rarely called anybody after that. I felt so alone at this point in my life. That letter broke me. I just about cried, and I had not cried since I was 12 years old. It hurt. It hurt. I just withdrew again. That was my way of dealing with things. Who could I talk to? I'm in prison. I can't talk to the other inmates and show my feelings. There weren't the kind of people on staff that I could talk to. They had put me on medication—medication for my bipolar disorder. I'm in prison. I don't have a family anymore. My mom is really upset with me. The old man doesn't care. Other than Bruce, I don't hear anything from my brothers and my sister. But Bruce was also in prison, and we communicated back and forth.

I didn't really regret what I had done to John Sander, but I really regretted what I had done to my mother. She had loved me and supported me through all my life, and she was really frustrated with me.

### MOVED TO FARIBAULT

After 13 months at Rush City, I was transferred again—this time to Faribault. Faribault was a level 3—medium security prison. Bruce was transferred to Stillwater—a level 5 prison. He was in for a second offense and had a higher security number. Faribault was a decent place with a big yard where we could walk around. There was a ball field for baseball, a good gym, good library. I had a TV in my cell. I decided to make the best of my situation. I applied for a job. I became a "swamper." That is the prison janitor. It paid 25 cents an hour. Other guys sneered at the pay, but I didn't do it for the money. I just wanted something to do. I kept the prison clean. I cleaned the lunchroom for the correctional officers. There were donuts that they let me eat. They treated me really, really decent.

### Noise was one of the worst things

Somehow my earlier enthusiasm for Christianity faded away. Christianity didn't seem the same down at Faribault. I tried not to think about the outside. I was in prison, and I had to adapt. The noise was one of the worst parts of prison. Prison is noisy about 20 hours a day. Prisoners are always shouting. It goes on all day and much of the night. The constant noise is very, very unnerving. At times you want to scream. There might be two prisoners in cells on opposite sides of the hall and different floors. They are playing chess and shouting their moves to each other—at two in the morning. It wakes you up. There are rules against this, but this is prison where the worst of the worst are gathered. Some guys think they are rap artists, and they are singing and carrying on. They don't follow rules very well.

I had countless hours to kill, and I killed a lot of them by reading. I read anything and everything. My favorites were Stephen King and Dean Koontz. I also liked some of the classics like Ernest Hemingway and John Steinbeck. If I had nothing else, I would read a romance novel. I never talked with other prisoners about my reading. They didn't give a shit.

I made some friends at Faribault. Geno was my best friend. He was doing "life on the installment plan." He was jailed again and again for a series of nonviolent offenses. He was about my size—maybe a little heavier at 260 or 270. Geno was of German descent, but he looked like a Mexican. He was a con man and a meth head. He was also a great guy—my best friend. His ex-wife was Patty. She later became my girlfriend, but that is another story. Another good friend was Tank. He was a little character—about 5'8", slender and scruffy looking. He was about my age—from the Cities. He was in for attempted murder. But he was carefree and very, very funny. He was working in maintenance at Faribault, and as the long Fourth of July weekend approached he removed an office air conditioner. He said he was going to get it cleaned, but he took it down to his cell and lived in air conditioned comfort for the three day weekend until he was discovered.

Tank got me into squirrels. There were squirrels out in the big yard. He trained them to take peanuts out of his pocket. I started training squirrels. I would yell at them and they would come running to me. I fed them crackers and stuff. It was something the guards couldn't take away from me. The animals liked me. I liked that. If somebody threw a rock at my squirrels, I got mad.

Tank and I took walks in the yard each afternoon. And each afternoon I would hear the faint sound of a train whistle. It was a familiar sound—a haunting sound. That train whistle reminded me of my best days of riding freight trains—the freedom of it all. I would let myself think for a few moments of that freedom—riding along across the open countryside with my bedroll and a bottle and some weed and a good book. I could almost feel the car swaying back and forth and hear the rhythmic clickity clack of the wheels. The sun would be on my face, and I was watching prairies and rivers go by. It was all beautiful. And I was free—free to do exactly what I pleased. Sometimes the whistle seemed to be calling me, "Fritz! Fritz!"

That freedom was the complete reverse of my present life. Here I was miserable and locked up in prison. What I was experiencing was somebody having complete control of me. I couldn't do what I wanted to do. I had always been one to do what I damn well pleased—ever since I was 14 years old. All of a sudden I was being told, "You can't do this. You can't do that." It was like culture shock to me. Somebody was telling me when to get up, when to go to sleep, when to do this, when to do that, when to eat, when to shower, when to watch TV, when not to watch TV. Lights out. Lights on. It was very, very hard for me to take. It was one of the two worst parts of prison—all the noise and being told what to do all the time. I loved that train whistle and all that it represented.

### I AM A GRANDFATHER

While I was in prison my sister Bev wrote to me and sent me a photo of my granddaughter. I learned that Jeremy had a daughter, had named her Hailey Maria, and she was born in 2000. She was now two years old. That's how I found out that I was a grandfather. My wife, Betty, didn't talk to anyone in the family except my dad. But Jeremy and Joshua were in contact with other members of my family. I looked at that photo of this beautiful little girl. She was my granddaughter. I wanted so badly to be the Grandpa that she deserved. But here I was sitting in prison.

**The photo of my first granddaughter, Hailey, that my mother sent to me when I was in prison.**

Unless you really screw up, it is typical to serve two thirds of the time of your sentence in prison and then be released for parole for the last third of the time. So for a long time I knew my release date. As that release date drew near I began to allow myself to think about what I would do as soon as I got out.

I have to admit that during my years in prison I didn't focus on doing something worthwhile or somehow reforming myself in prison. I didn't plan ahead. I didn't think much about the future. Likewise I didn't think much about what I was going to do when I was released. I didn't have a plan that said, I was going to get a job doing this, and I was going to put some money in the bank, quit drinking, do such and such to make my family proud of me, and then find my two sons and repair my relationship with them. I didn't think like that. First of all, I missed drinking, and I couldn't imagine myself never drinking again.

I can think of two things that I missed and thought about—a cigarette and a woman. I didn't torture myself with thinking about drinking because I knew that drinking was going to be forbidden during the year or so of my parole. But I thought about drawing in on a cigarette, and I thought about getting laid by a beautiful woman. I didn't think about any of my previous women. I had driven them all away. This would be someone new.

### I AM RELEASED FROM PRISON

As my release date came up, my friend Geno was already outside, and he offered to pick me up. He drove down to Faribault with his wife. I was released with nothing but the clothes on my back and $100 in cash. I was released at the front door, and there was Geno with hugs and a big smile. He had purchased a whole set of clothes for me—jeans, T shirt, shirt. He had a new jacket for me so I didn't have to wear the dumb blue prison jacket. He even gave me a new wallet. I felt just like a human being for the first time in a long while. It was great to get into those street clothes. Geno had been in and out enough times that he knew that a change of clothes would make me feel a helluva lot better. He introduced me to his wife Patty.

Then he gave me a ride up to my dad's place in Park Rapids. That was my parole address. You can't just be paroled. You had to give them a specific address. I didn't really want to stay at my dad's place, but I didn't have anywhere else to go.

Fortunately for me, his step-son worked at a lumberyard in Menahga just outside Park Rapids. He went to bat for me and asked the lumberyard manager if he would give me a job. He also talked to all the other workers and explained that I was an ex-con. The manager said OK, and I had a job waiting for me. I rode back and forth to work with this young man—the son of my dad's second wife.

As soon as I earned some money I moved out and got myself an apartment. Then I had several close calls. One night I was by myself, and I thought I would have a few beers. No one would know. The few beers immediately turned into a drunk, and the drunk lasted ten days. I was arrested and hauled back to prison. I was in Lino Lakes and then Rush City for five more months.

### "Intensive parole"

Then I was released once more—this time to "intensive parole" with an ankle bracelet. I was back at my dad's place, and the parole officer came to see me every day. I had a number of parole officers. They were all decent guys, but they could show up at any time day or night. They had more power than God. It was terrible to have to report to someone. I had to report in all the time.

My buddy Geno came up to visit me. He was doing meth and writing bad checks. I told him he better leave, but before he left the cops closed in and arrested him on the bad checks. The cops were sure I was part of the scheme. But my parole officer stood up for me. He said, "We know that John is not involved in this." Geno went to jail, and I was released.

Now I had only six weeks left on parole. I went out and got drunk. I smoked a bunch of meth and then a bunch of weed. After three days, I phoned my parole officer and told him what I had done. He said, "Where are you?"

I told him that I was putting myself into detox. He said, "We'll have you go through detox and then to the county jail." After a week in the jail, I was released, and my parole officer looked at me and said, "Look, John, you've got just a few weeks left. Just report in to me each day, OK? Make sure I know what's going on. You have less than a month to go. I'm not going to send you back to prison for that."

I finished my parole and left Minnesota.

# 8

# Trying to Quit

## Now I am labeled a "predatory offender"

As soon as I completed my parole, I left Minnesota. I was never a motorcycle rider, but all my brothers were. So I went out to Sturgis, South Dakota, for the Sturgis bike rally. I wanted to see what it was all about. It was noisy. Too noisy. I went to Rapid City, got drunk and was thrown in jail.

In jail they ran a background check and told me that I had to register as a sex offender. Apparently the state of Minnesota classified me as a "predatory offender" because of the kidnapping charges. I learned that there were three levels of offenders, and I was classified at Level I—the lowest level. Until the year 2024 I needed to fill out a form and return it.

I got out of jail in Rapid City, and I wound up in western Nebraska. I didn't really have any special destination. I rode a freight train across Nebraska and found myself in Council Bluffs, Iowa. I was walking east down Interstate 80—still no destination in mind.

## A Bus Ticket to Bangor and Stephen King

A truck stopped, and the trucker said, "Where are you going?"

I wasn't going anywhere in particular, but for some reason I blurted out "Bangor, Maine." Just to name some place.

We got to talking, and he said, "I'm going on to Chicago, but let me buy you a bus ticket."

I thought he was going to buy me a bus ticket to Chicago. But he drove me to Chicago, drove his semi to the bus terminal and bought me a bus ticket to Bangor, Maine. So, I found myself on this Greyhound bus heading for Maine. I had never been there, and I thought it would be an adventure, but I was really uncomfortable on the bus. There were a lot of foreign people on the bus speaking languages I didn't understand. I was sitting there—dirty and stinky. I needed a shower. I didn't have much money, so I didn't have a bottle with me. I was shaky and sick with the DT's. I just laid in my seat for the two and a half days to get me to Bangor. A bus was not my cup of tea. You can't smoke cigarettes. You can't drink on a bus the way I like to drink, so I didn't drink at all.

I got off the bus at the Bangor bus station, and there was a bar right next door. So I went into this bar and lit up a cigarette.

"No. You can't do that!"

I found out this was a nonsmoking bar. But I got to talking to people. They wondered what the hell I was doing. "Where are you from? You've got a funny accent."

I met a few people. They told me that Stephen King drank in that bar on a regular basis. I asked, "Where does he live?"

One fellow pointed up the hill, "There are two mansions at the top of that hill. He lives in one and bought the other to restore."

I announced, "Well, I'm going to go visit him." Here was my favorite author less than a mile away. Of course I was drunk. I walked up the hill and banged on his door. No answer. No answer. So I went back to the bar.

Someone at the end of the bar said, "Oh, he's off on a book signing tour right now. Otherwise he would have answered the door. He's just a regular guy. You would never know that he was world famous."

I missed my chance to meet Stephen King. But I hung around Bangor for a week or two.

Everything seemed so closed in—all the trees and everything. I had been through New York and Boston filled with all these people, and now I was in Maine filled with all these trees. I slept along the railroad tracks. There was a little camp there. You could see that somebody had lived there recently. But there weren't many homeless people in Bangor.

I got tired of Maine. I felt claustrophobic. I stayed in Maine a couple weeks I figured there would be a few compadres around there, but I couldn't find any. I slept under the stars. Sometimes I slept under bridges. I got inspired to see Bar Harbor, but I never made it.

### Smoking meth and writing tickets for the St. Paul police department

At Thanksgiving time I was sleeping under a bridge in Sioux Falls, South Dakota. I phoned my old friend Geno. He happened to have his son-in-law's Cadillac and a bunch of meth. He said, "I'll come and get you. Where are you?" I told him, and he drove from Minneapolis to Sioux Falls to pick me up. Geno drove me to his place in St. Paul. It was the day after Thanksgiving in 2005. Geno and I hung out together for a couple of weeks in St. Paul where he was living at the time with his girlfriend.

Geno's ex-wife Patty began calling me. She also lived in St. Paul and invited me over. I met Patty a year earlier when Geno picked me up at the front door of Faribault prison. Patty had come with Geno down to Faribault. She was short and a little heavy. She was young—seven years younger than I. She had black hair. Patty had bad teeth for years, so she never smiled. But she liked to laugh and have a good time. Soon Patty and I were having a lot of fun together—just hanging out, talking. She was very funny. She told me that she smoked so much meth during the 90's that she was awake for the entire decade.

Geno had introduced me to meth. I had done crack years earlier, but I had stayed away from hard drugs for years. I just drank. But when Geno introduced me to meth, I liked it right away. It was better than weed. I fell in love with it.

Anyway when I visited Patty, she was still doing meth, and I joined her. I started smoking meth out of a bubble. This was a glass tube with a round bubble at the end. You put the meth in there and heated the bubble. When it melted, you smoked it. That was my preferred way of doing meth.

Anyway Pat and I were hanging out together. We got a real bad snowstorm. The snow emergency lanes were filled with parked cars. I saw a perfect opportunity. I applied at the city office for a job writing tickets. They immediately put me to work. They gave me a St. Paul city badge number so that I was official, and I walked to the snow emergency route and started writing tickets. I laughed at the situation. I was only a few months out of parole, and here I was—writing tickets with a St. Paul police badge number. Of course, I neglected to tell them I was an ex-con. They never checked.

It was a good gig, and I was good at it. I would work for 12 hours, take a few hours off and then return to work. I wrote hundreds of tickets. I especially loved putting tickets on the fanciest cars.

We had several big snowstorms that winter, and each time I returned to my duties—writing tickets. In the meantime Patty and I were getting close. We smoked meth, and we talked and talked. We talked about everything—about our childhoods, our kids, what our dreams were. Then she had two kids. Next things you know, we were sleeping together.

I really liked her. I loved her humor. She took an interest in me. She wanted to know about me. I loved that. It had been a while. I had just served four and a half years in prison where nobody gave a shit . I had some friends in prison, but nobody like Patty.

Patty understood prison because Geno had been in and out of prison. She understood some of the thinking of felons. She had been divorced from Geno for a few years, but they always stayed in contact with each other. They were able to continue being friends. Now I was living with her. I had not planned on that.

Somehow Patty really understood me. She told me, "I knew when we got into this relationship that you ran. You needed to be set free from time to time. I have no problem with that." She knew enough about me to know that somebody could not tell me what to do. You can't tie me down. I would get very restless, and I would have to go. In the past I had to create fights and things like that for a reason to leave.

But Patty said, "You don't have to create a fight with me. If you want to leave, all you have to do is tell me you are going and go."

### I visit my sons; I blow it

Between 2005 and 2010 I spent a lot of time with Patty, but I also took trips out West. On one of those trips I got ahold of Josh somehow. I knew I had a grandbaby. I got her picture three years earlier when I was in prison. I don't know how many times I looked at that photo of Hailey. Now I wanted to see her.

Josh had given me his phone number. We had been communicating back and forth when I was on parole. We had civil conversations. He lived in Hawaii for a few years, and then he moved back to Portland. I knew they all lived in the same area of Portland. So, one day I just decided, "I'm going to Oregon."

All my buddies in St. Paul had told me, "When you get ready to go someplace, let us know. We want to go with you. We want to go ride a freight train." But none of them would go. I asked a couple guys if they wanted to go out West with me, but nobody would. It was springtime. It was nice weather. Every spring I would get an urge to go. As soon as it started getting nice, I would get this urge to go.

So I took a freight train out to the West Coast. I was drinking pretty heavy. That is the time that I had a cell phone. I was able to call Josh when I got to Portland. He came and picked me up. I was grubby –dirty and filthy when he picked me up. The first thing I had to do was bum a pair of socks from him. I didn't have clean socks. Josh and I started smoking weed together. He was in his early 20's at that time, and he was living with his cousin.

After a few days Josh arranged for Jeremy to come over and bring Hailey. He was going to bring Hailey over so I could meet her. Then he would take us all out to eat. It sounded wonderful, and it sounded scary. I was scared. I hadn't seen Jeremy in 13 or 14 years and now he had this little girl. Jeremy had an early drinking problem, but now he was sober. He was so upset to learn that I was still drinking.

I started out that morning with just a few beers to calm my nerves. Those few beers turned into more beers and then more beers. We were supposed to meet at 3 o'clock, and suddenly it was time. By now I was pretty drunk. I decided that I better not go see them when I was drunk. So, I didn't go.

I talked to Jeremy a couple days later. He drove over. We met. In the car neither of us said much. He picked me up and drove me across the river over to the freight yard in Vancouver, Washington. I knew I could get an eastbound out of there. He gave me $50 and told me, "Go away and don't come back."

So, now both of my sons had told me, "Go away and don't come back." It hurt me so bad. There was nothing I could do to change things. I had been out there. I had my opportunity. I thought, "I'll never see my boys or my grandkids again. I never got to see Hailey. Oh, man. I just blew it. I'm never going to see my kids." I finally had the opportunity. And what did I do? I went out and drank it away again. I hurt. Oh, I hurt. I was so disgusted with myself. I headed back to Minnesota on a freight train. It was a really hard ride—coming back to Minnesota. I had just ruined my one chance with my kids.

During all those years when I didn't know where my boys were, my nephews had always told me, "Your sons are going to get ahold of you. They will find you. Don't worry, Uncle John." But now they finally did get ahold of me, and I went out to Oregon and blew it. So I had a lot of suicidal thinking on that ride back. It was a very hard ride alone.

### Living in a camp in St. Paul

So I got back to St. Paul, and I was camped out in Maplewood just north of St. Paul. I had various camp mates. My best buddy was Cherokee. We became really, really good friends. Cherokee claimed he was Indian, but I wasn't so sure. He was from the Carolinas. He used to work at the Juel Fairbanks halfway house. He had stayed sober for 10 years, and he was working at this halfway house. But then Cherokee started drinking and smoking crack and he wound up back out on the streets.

Cherokee's most distinguishing feature was that he had no teeth. He bit off food and chewed it with his gums. He could chew any old thing with his gums. He even gummed peanuts. Cherokee had long hair and a straggly beard. He was five or six years older than I. He was a wonderful guy to hang out with. I slept outside. So did Cherokee. We didn't believe in missions. Occasionally when it got really, really cold, we tried to find somebody with an apartment where we could sleep on the floor. Cherokee and I spent the full winter outside in Maplewood. It was the winter of 2006—2007. We lived outside that whole time. We had a couple of pretty bad storms that year.

Cherokee and I would find camps in inconspicuous places behind buildings, behind groves of trees. The first key is to find a location that is hidden. That's the first and most important thing. You want a place where people don't see you—where you can have a little fire and not attract attention. Behind a grove of trees was really good.

Second, you want to be able to get in and out of there without being noticed. As soon as people start seeing you, they call the cops, and you get chased off again. We had a really nice camp back behind the Rainbow Grocery Store in Maplewood where you really couldn't see us. It was away from the buildings. There was only one little spot where you could see a house light. But that was across the swamps, and we didn't worry about that.

Third, you want a camp that is pretty close to two things—a public bathroom that you can use and a really good place to fly a sign.

We set up a six-man tent, and Cherokee had his own private little tent because he was a "pissticle." He pissed all over himself when he was drunk, and in the winter time it turned into an icicle. So, we called him a "pissticle." We wouldn't let him sleep in the tent with us.

There was a laundromat nearby. The owner used to have a bar down by the mission, and she got to know homeless people. She let us come into her laundromat. Actually Cherokee and I slept in that laundromat on nights when it was really, really cold. We would come over before closing time, and when she closed up for the day, she would lock us in for the night. She was one of those really, really nice people.

Once you have a good spot, you set up your camp. A good camp has a good toilet hole. You dig a hole 30 feet or more away from camp. Preferably you don't shit out there because you might step in it. You do that in grocery store bathrooms, gas stations—places like that. At that camp we had raccoons coming into our camp. Baby raccoons would come in and clean up all our chicken bones. We would put stuff in the coolers.

The layout of the camp was a tent with some lawn chairs set up around a small fire pit. I slept in my bedroll—no air mattress or anything—right on the ground—usually not in the tent because there were stinky bodies in the tent. We set up a couple of Igloo coolers. We tried to keep ice in one of the coolers. Every day we were out flying signs, so we were pulling in enough money that we were able to drink decent. There were often four of us together, and between the four of us we were making at least $50 or $75 a day. We would take turns flying our signs. The four of us lived on $50 to $75 a day when necessary. Of course, some days we would bring back $300 in a day. That's when I would go and buy some meth. I would say, "Ok, I got enough. I'll go get some meth." Everybody liked meth.

Our tent was in the trees. It kind of blended in. We didn't worry about somebody stealing or trashing our camp during the day. There was a trail in to the camp, but it was pretty tough to get in. It was one long trail. We didn't tell anybody about our camp. I don't know how the cops ever found it. We were about 100 yards behind the parking lot down this long trail through the trees. We were down a hill, hidden in the woods. I don't know how anyone ever saw us back there.

We tried to have a radio, but they always broke right away. You go to the pawn shop and buy yourself a radio. Within a couple of days it's broken. So we just sat around the fire chattering and talking—bullshitting each other. I had lots of stories. People liked listening to my stories. We had a fire pit, and we kept a fire going. We sat around and drank until the wee hours of the morning. When we were smoking meth, we didn't sleep at all.

When Cherokee and I had this camp, there was this cop from White Bear Lake who came to check on us. He was an old sergeant in the police force. I can't remember his name now, but he came and checked on us. He made sure we weren't frozen—that we were OK. One time he brought a rookie back there, and told him, "These guys are really cool guys. They ain't bothering anybody. You just want to make sure they are OK."

### SAVED BY THE TOOTH FAIRY

It was probably 2007. Patty and I had a fight. It started when I called her Dorothy—an old girlfriend of mine. Patty knew that

I didn't think that Dorothy was a good person. So, she resented being called Dorothy. She got mad, and we had an argument. So I left. I had been gone for two weeks before I decided to come back. Now I was walking over to her place. It was a summer night, nine or ten o'clock, getting dark. I was sitting in this little park a couple blocks from her house. I was just sitting there, minding my own business, drinking a bottle of wine. All of a sudden a bunch of little kids came around. One shouted, "What's an old man doing in a park unless he's a child molester?" They started throwing rocks at me. It was a group of about ten little black kids ranging in age from 9 to about 15.

I was a little annoyed, but didn't think much about it. I just got up and started walking away. They followed me. I was a block away from a bar, so I walked to the bar. Now I was just a half block from Patty's house. There were two gals sitting outside the bar smoking a cigarette. The next thing I knew I was hit from behind with something. I went down. It's hard to knock me down with one punch. But that must have been a pipe or something. I was flat on the ground, and they were kicking me from all four directions.

Then the girls came running and shouting, "Leave that guy alone." At the same time a black guy who was driving by, stopped his car in the middle of the street, jumped out and chased these kids off of me.

I was bleeding and spitting blood. One of the girls waved down a cop who happened to be on patrol in the neighborhood. "We just witnessed this guy getting assaulted."

The cop stopped the car, leaned out his window, looked at my backpack, stayed in the car and then he looked at me and said, "I ain't got time." Those were his exact words, "I ain't got time." He drove away real slowly.

The girls shouted at the cop to come back, but he drove away. I was on the ground spitting blood all over the place. I finally got up and walked to Patty's place. I got into Patty's house and put a cigarette in my mouth, and it fell out. I couldn't hold a cigarette in my mouth. My jaw was flapping around. I said I wanted to go to sleep but Patty insisted that I go to the hospital. She had some friends who had a car, and they drove me to the emergency room at Regions Hospital. I wasn't bleeding that much, but I was spitting blood. I didn't realize how bad it was. Of course, I was pretty drunk.

I got to that emergency room, and they immediately got me into a hospital gown. They gave me some pills to knock me out. The very next morning I was in the operating room. Dr. Derek Schmidt was the main doctor. He was a young guy. He went in through the inside of my mouth and found that I had my jaw broken in three places. He put in three plates to hold my jaw together. Then he wired my jaw shut. He had a very good bedside manner. He had a sense of humor. I never dealt with a doctor with a bedside manner like his. I really liked him.

After I healed a little, I was dismissed from the hospital and I went back to stay with Patty. I couldn't eat solid food, of course, so I blended everything up in a blender and sucked it through a straw. I ate what everybody else ate. I just drank it through a straw. I only lost about five pounds. I remembered my mom blending up food when my brother Bob got his jaw busted. He managed just fine with a blender and a straw. I did the same thing.

But my jaw wouldn't heal. Dr. Schmidt said, "I'm not happy with what I did." He did another surgery, and this time he came from the outside of my face. Then he replaced these metal plates and rewired my jaw.

With my jaws wired shut, I returned to my straw diet. But then, in my infinite wisdom, I jumped on a freight train. In Utah the railroad police caught me and threw me in jail. The charge was trespassing, riding on a freight train. Now I was locked behind bars with my jaw wired shut. Through my clenched teeth I tried to explain that I needed a special diet. The jailers ignored me. I didn't eat for two days until they finally let me see a doctor. I told the doctor about the jaw and that I had to get back to Minnesota for a medical appointment to have the wires removed. "The appointment is in St. Paul in a week. I need to be back in St. Paul."

The doctor was skeptical. He said, "Well, we'll see about this." The jail faxed a message to Regions Hospital in St. Paul asking for my medical records. Regions faxed back a big pile of reports describing my injury and my surgeries. When the Utah jail saw the reports, they released me. They didn't want me staying in their jail requiring expensive surgery. It would have cost them a lot of money. So, with my jaw still wired shut, I jumped on a train to head back to Minnesota. During the ride back I drank everything through a straw. Of course I drank a lot.

**When I regained consciousness after the jaw surgery, I found that the tooth fairy had left me a small bottle containing my tooth and a dollar bill.**

Back in St. Paul I saw Dr. Schmidt again. When I told him I had been riding a freight train with my wired jaw, he just shook his head at me. "What is wrong with you?" But he never screamed or hollered at me. He was just really a cool, cool guy.

Dr. Schmidt said my jaw still wasn't healing. He said they were going to go in a third time. They might take a piece of my hip bone and fuse that to my jaw They were afraid the jaw was dying. He put me out for a third surgery. But when I woke up from that surgery there was a little glass jar by my bed. Inside that glass jar was a tooth and a dollar bill.

When Doc Schmidt came in that morning, he was smiling. He explained that one of my teeth was right where the break was. That tooth kept moving, and this was preventing the jaw from setting. So he removed the tooth. He gestured to the bottle with the tooth and the dollar bill and said, "That's from the tooth fairy."

Now my jaw healed. He gave me oxycodone for pain. At the same time I was drinking and smoking meth. I was never in any pain.

### Good friends and decent cops

One of my camp buddies was "Third Eye." He was called that because at one point he had a swastika tattooed on his forehead. Later he had the tattoo changed into an "eye." So, we called him "Third Eye." I didn't spend much time in downtown St. Paul. I didn't go to missions. But I was around there enough to get to know the twins—Val and Irene. They were Natives—living on the street and drinking hard. They were about 40. They were just beautiful girls. They died a year apart. They drank themselves to death.

One night there was a bunch of us underneath a bridge at Interstate 694 and White Bear Avenue. There was Cherokee, Tommy Two Tokes, Don, several others and me. One of the guys was getting mouthy. He was messing with my buddy Don. Don was a little guy, so I walked over and told the mouthy guy, "If you want to fuck with somebody, fuck with me." The next thing you know this guy and I were rolling around on the ground. I was on top of him, and I was hitting him, but this guy would not quit fighting. I kept hitting him, and I was wearing myself out. He wouldn't give up. I was afraid I would kill him. Finally I felt a hand grabbing my shoulder. It was a cop. The cop stopped the fight right there.

He said, "Alright, what the hell is going on here?"

I said, "Sir, it's just a personal matter here."

The cop seemed to think for a moment. Then he asked the four who were not in the fight, "Well, which one of these two guys do you want gone?" Everybody pointed at the other guy, so the cops hauled him away. They didn't want to go through the hassle and the paperwork in arresting all of us. He was a decent cop and took a common sense approach. One of these guys is a trouble maker in the group. Remove that guy and let the rest of the group continue on with their party.

### I try to quit drinking

Oftentimes I tried to sober up. I was there in St. Paul for five or six years, and I made several attempts. I went to a few AA meetings. I would get to disliking myself so bad that something had to change. But AA wasn't for me. I thought they were a bunch of phonies. I would go 20 or 30 days without drinking. I did that two or three times. Then I would start drinking again for no particular reason.

One time after I had been at an AA meeting, I got myself a quart of vodka. I was going to do some "controlled drinking." It was kind of an experiment. I wanted to see if I could control my drinking. So, I drank about half that bottle of vodka. For me that was about two drinks, and half the bottle was gone. Then I put that quart bottle away. It was still half full. But all I could think about was the rest of that booze. I struggled and fought. That worked for about ten days. I looked at the half filled bottle, but I didn't touch it day after day. But all I could think about each day was that bottle with good vodka in it. I knew I had that bottle. It was kind of a security blanket. I got the DT's and started shaking.

Finally, I decided, "Ok. I'm going to drink that other half. I have learned that I can do that. I can quit drinking. I can succeed at this controlled drinking." Well, I drank that other half, and I couldn't quit. That set me off on my last drunk.

### I am reaching the end

I found myself in Laurel, Montana. Now I was having super anxiety attacks. It felt like I was having a heart attack. My heart was racing. My mind was racing too. I couldn't get back on a train. The more I thought about it, the worse my anxiety became.

At the time I was staying with a woman who went by the name "C.C. Rider." She phoned my dad. He drove from Minnesota to Montana and picked me up. He hauled me back to his home in Park Rapids, Minnesota. I was restless. I couldn't stay with my dad. I went back to Fargo, then to the Twin Cities. There I stayed with Patty, but I couldn't settle down. I moved back outside and slept under bridges.

I was very, very depressed. It was the early part of 2010. I was 50 years old and homeless. I had been homeless off and on ever since I was 16. I had 12 DWI's. I had been in jail in 16 different states. I couldn't stay out of trouble. In the last 34 years I had spent four years in the state penitentiary and a total of about four years in various jails. I couldn't quit drinking. Every time I drank, I drank until I was drunk. I did various drugs—weed, meth, heroin. I had been to chemical treatment centers 16 times, but nothing worked.

I had driven away my friends. I was estranged from the family I grew up in, and I was estranged from my wife and two sons. I had grandchildren I had never seen and probably never would see. I was reaching the end.

# 9

# Recovery

## Mental Health Unit

I walked down to the Union Gospel Mission on the north side of St. Paul. It was 8 or 9 o'clock on a cool April evening. I met this black chaplain. He was a heavy set guy and very, very friendly. He was easy to talk to. I told him that I was thinking about killing myself. I said, "I'm done. I am just thoroughly done with life." I sat and talked to him for about a half hour about how depressed I was. He finally talked me into going up to St. Paul's Regions Hospital. He took me over to the emergency room in his car.

They started giving me Valium in the emergency room. They saw me starting to shake. They found room for me right away in their mental health unit. They kept me fully drugged for about four days. They had me up in the unit and kept feeding me Valium. I was liking it. I was thinking it wasn't so bad to be sober. But you're not really sober. It's alcohol in a pill form.

I was getting more and more withdrawn as I sat in this mental health unit. They had different classes throughout the day. I tried to get involved in these classes. There were classes on "How to handle stress"—different things like that. They had an art class and recreation. I tried to get involved, but I was very withdrawn.

A social worker started talking to me. She suggested alcohol treatment. I said, "Naw, I'm not going. I'm not going back to another treatment center. It's a waste of time."

I talked to the psychiatrist, and she mentioned my depression. Her records showed that this was my third visit to their mental health unit in two years. She mentioned electric shock therapy for my depression. I said, "No. Uh uh. I ain't doin' no shock therapy." So, this social worker, a young gal, good looking gal—probably 30 years old, just had a baby—she started talking to me more. I was getting more and more upset. I just walked out one day.

I was going to AMA out. AMA stands for "against medical advice." I had checked myself in. I thought I could check myself out. So I told them I wanted to AMA out, and they said, "No. We're putting a 72-hour hold on you right now. You are in no shape to go anywhere." They threatened to commit me, which meant I would end up in a state hospital or something. I didn't want to go back to a state hospital. I had done that in Fergus Falls. So, I started going along with them.

They got me back on my medication, and I started mellowing out. They offered again for me to go to treatment. This time I said I would go. I agreed because I knew that I could walk out the door of the treatment center. I would no longer be locked up. I was in a locked mental health unit at the time.

### 28 DAYS IN TREATMENT

So, I decided, OK. I'll go to the treatment center. I'll find out what it's like. I got there, and I didn't have cigarettes, I didn't have anything. I had no clothes with me. Patty brought me some stuff. That was the only time she came to see me. I was there for 28 days, and it was the only visit I had.

I started bumming cigarettes from other patients, and they turned out to be a bunch of really decent people. The staff was also pleasant to be around. I was in the Regions' ADAP Treatment Center. ADAP stands for "Alcohol and Drug Addiction Program."

It got to be evening of that first day, and I couldn't make up my mind what to do. I was between a rock and a hard place. Do I leave or do I stay? I was thinking about walking away. What good is this going to do? I had been through 16 treatments. What's the point of going through another treatment?

That's when I got on my hands and knees. I said a prayer to something. I had no clue what God was. All I said was, "I can't do this anymore." That's all I said. I decided to stay in treatment. That's when I realized that I was no longer thinking about drinking. I'm not sure whether it was that I had made up my mind that I'd had enough or whether it was something to do with this prayer. I'd like to think it was a little bit of both. Perhaps there is something out there that gives a shit about us.

So I really got involved in treatment. I did all the paperwork. I only felt like leaving one time after that. I just about left because one person who worked there wasn't a very pleasant lady. She started bitching at me about something. I reacted. I told her "Fuck you" and started walking away. But I didn't have anywhere to go.

Soon I was finishing up my 28-day treatment, and I still had no place to go. With my record it was really, really hard to find any place that would take me. As soon as they saw that phrase "predatory offender" they said, "Oh, no. We can't have you in here." I checked out four or five different places before I found the Greenhouse here in St. Paul. They said I could come there.

I got there, and I thought it was just a sober house where I could live and do my thing. I quickly learned that everybody around me was drinking, smoking weed and stealing. I thought, "What good is this? I can't listen to these people."

### Staying with Patty

So, I called Patty and asked her if I could stay with her for a little bit. She said yeah. So I moved over there. I thought, the only way

I was going to stay sober from here was to get really involved in something. So I started going to AA. I found a group called "Main Idea." They met in the downtown Al-Anon Club. It was a big group of people. They had 20 or 25 meetings a week. They started at 7:30 in the morning. They had noon meetings. They had three in the afternoon meetings and more in the evenings. So, there was no excuse not to make a meeting. I went to meetings three or four times a day. That first year of sobriety, I probably went to a thousand meetings. I had been so involved in drinking that I had to replace that drinking with something else. I knew that I needed to fill that time. So, I hung out at this Al-Anon Club. I went to meetings. There was drinking and smoking meth at Patty's house. I knew it wasn't doing me any good to be there. But at the time I had no other place to go.

### American House

After about six or seven months of being sober, an AA friend named George told me about the American House. He was living there and recommended it to me. He told me, "Talk to Suzanne Jarrett at the American House." He introduced us. I talked to Suzanne, and she really cared. I felt like this woman really, really cared. She was interested in what was going on in me. She turned out to be a wonderful woman.

Suzanne was blonde, about 5'6." She was very soft-spoken. She asked me questions to bring me out of myself. Then she listened. She told me, "We're going to get you in here." That's the first thing she said to me. "We're going to get you in here."

I thought, "Lord, maybe I can get a place here of my own." I had no idea what the rooms or facilities were like. I just knew that it was a place that I could call my own. So, I started applying to get in. I got turned down. It was because of my arrest record. Nobody wants to house a predatory offender, even if it is not a sexual case. You are included right in with that group of people. So, this went on for three months. They said "No."

But Suzanne said, "Let's not quit. Let's appeal this." So, we appealed. She kept encouraging me. "We're going to do this, John. We'll find you a place."

Finally, I went in there one day and she said, "Good news. You've been accepted." Tears just about came to my eyes. I'm going to have a place of my own. The only thing I had to do was go through this place they call "The Blue House." I had to spend a few days there before I could transition into the American House.

I was there only a few days, but I got bed bugs. It was the only time in my life that I caught bed bugs. So, I brought bed bugs with me to American House. I was embarrassed. "How good does this look? I just moved in, and I've got bed bugs with me." I found a few of them, and I reported them right away. They fumigated the room, and there was no problem after that. But I thought, "Good Lord, I start out by bringing in bed bugs."

So here I was. I had this room—about 10' x 15' with brick walls and 12' ceilings. It was an old warehouse. I was on the third floor with a nice corner room looking out at the street to the southwest. It was a nice looking place. The room had a big closet, and you could see these big exposed wooden beams. There was even an elevator. The only thing was—the windows didn't open. They had central air, so they didn't want the windows to open. It was furnished with a bed and a desk with a chair for the desk. That's all. So, I started looking for a dresser and sheets and blankets and all that stuff. I needed everything. I didn't have anything.

Suzanne helped me find bedding at People Incorporated. She worked with the Beacon Interfaith Housing Collaborative people who owned and ran the apartment building. The next thing you know I have bedding and a coffee pot. I was excited about the coffee pot. I had become addicted to coffee.

Stuff was donated to me. I had a room of my own. It was nice and cool due to the air conditioning. I was high styling it. The bathroom was right across the hall from me, and the kitchen was next door. In the kitchen each of us had our own dorm refrigerator, and each had its own padlock. I also had my own cupboard. It was about 12" x 24". I kept a lock on that. I had some pots and pans that I kept in my room. I always washed them up right after I got done using them. There was no sink or running water in the room itself. There were three bathrooms with shower or tub on each floor. There were plenty of bathroom facilities. I never had a problem getting access to the bathroom. They had a cleaning crew that came in and cleaned the bathrooms and communal areas each week. We were responsible for our own rooms.

I remember cooking my first meal. I was standing at the stove realizing that I only had to take care of myself. I didn't have to worry about feeding anybody else. I didn't have to worry about food. I had stuff in my fridge. That first night I made myself a hamburger—a cheeseburger actually and some ramen noodles. The ramen noodles were cheap. I took my supper back to my room. I was wishing I had a TV. I don't think I had a radio yet either.

So I was sitting at my desk—eating. I started thinking—there are some things that I needed to get—a radio or a TV to keep myself sane. There were times sitting in that room that reminded me of a prison cell. Of course I wasn't locked up. But I have to admit that sometimes the room would start closing in on me.

When they gave me the key to my room, it had a fob on it. I didn't know what a fob was. I didn't have any idea that it would open my door. To get in, I had an actual key to my room. I had never had a key. Even when I was married, I didn't have keys to where I lived. So, this was the first house key that I ever had. It's really weird to realize that I had a room with a key. I could get away from people. I could lock people out. I didn't have to be around people using and drinking. I was so grateful. I was SO grateful.

It wasn't noisy at the American House. There was some noise. You would have people who sometimes turned their stereo up really loud, but mostly people were pretty respectful. They didn't want to get kicked out. They would kick you out for too much partying and different things. No one wanted to be kicked out of the American House.

### I don't go to the family gathering

That first year that I was sober, there was a family gathering up in McIntosh. My mother, sister and brothers invited me again. I used to stay away from family gatherings before when I was too drunk. This first year I thought I was too sober to go. I didn't remember how to behave with these people. I didn't know how to handle myself sober. I needed to learn these things.

### AA first steps

I learned that AA has 12 steps which are very good guidelines for life. If everybody lived by those 12 steps, it would be a much better world. I needed to learn them. I started at the beginning. For me it all started with step 1. I accepted the fact that I was helpless with alcohol. I had to admit that I was beat. I was flat beat. That is when I got down on my knees and said, "I'm done. I can't do this anymore. Step 2 calls for us to "come to believe that a power greater than ourselves could restore us to sanity." I had to believe in something outside myself. In a sense that was hard for me, but I used AA as that "power outside me." Because I had seen AA sober up so many people. I knew that there was something to that power.

Step 3 tells us to "make a decision to turn our will and our lives over to the care of God as we understand Him." That meant I should turn my life over to the care of God as I understood him. Here you are saying, "OK. I'm going to do it your way. I am no longer going to try to do it my way because my way has not worked." In a way I did the first three steps that first day when I got down on my knees. That wasn't so hard.

I learned that when you are starting out in AA, you ask someone to be your sponsor. It should be someone you feel comfortable with. I asked Steve my AA friend to be my sponsor. He agreed. He had been sober and in AA for the past 32 years. He was about my age, and he remembered his early days of sobriety as if they were yesterday. I phoned him almost every day in that first year, and he was always ready to stop what he was doing and talk with me. The key was that Steve was gentle with me. Previously in treatment centers I had these hard core people who always wanted to push things down my throat, but Steve was different. He would let me come to my own conclusions on things. Most generally, it was the right conclusion. I just had to work my way to it by talking it through.

He helped me reach my own conclusions by prodding me with questions. He spent a lot of time listening. I would talk, and I'd talk and I'd talk. Finally I would come full circle and realize that I had the answer to start with.

I used to think I could jump around in those 12 steps, but I learned that I couldn't. My sponsor helped me take each step one after another in order. It took me three months to do steps 4 and 5. Step four is: "Make a searching and moral inventory of yourself." This gets to the real meat of the stuff. You sit down and take a real look at yourself—the good and the bad. I started to realize that how you react to things matters. I had some things to work on. Before that I was just stumbling around. I found out that I am really a selfish, self-centered person. I strive not to be selfish any more. I try to listen to other people.

Step 5 is you have to admit to God and to yourself and to another human being the exact nature of your wrongs. I did this with my sponsor. Some people choose to do this with their minister.

### Making amends

Step 9 was hard for me. It says: "Make direct amends to such people wherever possible, except when to do so would injure them or others." I had to start preparing myself to make amends to people. A lot of them aren't happy to see your face. Making amends can be a very tough thing to do. Sometimes you get rejected. Only one person really rejected me when I was trying to say I'm sorry to them. It hurt me.

My wife was a special case. She wouldn't talk to me. I wanted to talk to this woman. I wanted to tell her that it wasn't just her fault, and it wasn't just my fault. It went both ways, but I had been very wrong. I didn't blame my wife for staying away from me. I really didn't. I would like to tell her that. That she hid my children from me is another story.

Making amends is generally a pretty good thing to do. I talked to my brother Bob. I owed him a bunch of money. He had forgotten about it. This had bothered me for 25 years. He forgot about it years ago. He said he didn't even remember until I brought it up to him.

Making amends is kind of a selfish thing because you are clearing yourself, but it also states "make direct amends wherever possible except when to do so would injure them or others." You can't clear your conscience by hurting somebody else.

I had a former girlfriend up in Thief River—Diane. We had a rocky relationship. I lived with her and didn't live with her, lived with her and then didn't live with her. I owed her money. I just left. I walked away one day. I never said a word. I just left everything. I left and went down to South Dakota.

Finally, after I sobered up, I called her. It was 2013. I apologized for my behavior and asked her how much money I owed her. She said, "John, I lost that house anyway. It's gone." She didn't care that I owed her anything. She said, "It's OK." We have seen each other a few times since then. But now we are able to have a civilized conversation. It was a relief for me to realize that I hadn't really ruined that friendship.

### I become a sponsor

After I had been sober for a year or 15 months, a guy named Pat walked up to me and said, "Will you sponsor me?" He was a younger guy, a real successful businessman. He still had all his cars and his boats—all that stuff. He came to me who didn't have anything, and asked me to sponsor him. I was terrified of this. What have I got to give this guy? I was overwhelmed. So I went to my sponsor and said, "What am I going to do?"

He said, "Well, you've just become a sponsor." So, then I told Pat that I would work with him. All I could do is tell him what had worked for me in staying sober these last 15 months. I told him what I did: 1. Don't drink. 2. Get involved in something. I got involved in AA. You have to replace the time you spent drinking and carrying on with something else. When I started sponsoring people, I did the same thing that my sponsor did with me. I spent a lot of time listening. It's important that you can hear what they are saying. Then let them hear what they are saying. So many times, we know our own answers.

### AA people

I run across people in St. Paul all the time that I know from AA. There are more people in AA than you realize. There is a tight knit bond in AA because you are all struggling with the same thing. You are all striving for that sobriety.

People in AA have only one thing in common. They are all alcoholics. People who are not in AA, I call them "normies." Most AA people are very outgoing and loud. We are not a dull lot. We have fun. We can laugh at things that most people will cry about such as my 12th DWI. I was driving to the court hearing for my 11th DWI in northern Minnesota, and I got pulled over and received my 12th DWI. In fact I couldn't make the court hearing because now I was in a different county jail—this time for my 12th DWI.

When most people hear this they shake their head in shock or exasperation. They say, "Oh, man!" But when AA people hear about that, they just laugh. AA people understand it. It was the alcohol and my obsession to drink.

AA people are also a very honest bunch. We have to be. AA people tend to be very sensitive people in a lot of ways. They drank to cover their feelings. I covered my feelings for 38 years—by drinking and doing drugs. I never learned how to feel. These last years I have been learning how to feel. At first when I sobered up I would take things really personal. Somebody would say something to me, and I would feel really guilty. I still struggle today with learning how to feel.

### Mental illness

In April of 2010 I had been on and off meds since the early 90's. I would take my meds. I would stay sober, and I would get to feeling really good. Then I quit taking my meds. Within months I would be drinking again. I wasn't accurately diagnosed as bipolar until a couple years after I quit drinking – in 2012. Prior to 2012 my meds were for depression and anxiety. Now I am on a mood stabilizer too. It helps my bipolar disorder because it prevents me from bouncing up and down.

I sometimes think I don't need to be on these meds anymore. But then I remember my past experience—when I quit my meds, I start drinking. Prior to 2012 I only took two meds. Bupropion is purely for depression, and Celexa is for depression as well as minimizing anxiety attacks. I sometimes got anxiety attacks when I went grocery shopping. I got my grocery cart full of groceries, and then my heart would start racing. I would feel like I was having a heart attack. I would just about freeze up. I was trying to make decisions—what to get and what not to get. Then I would be surrounded by people, and it seemed like they were all pushing and shoving. I was so used to being alone, that when I was in this situation, I couldn't deal with it. I would leave my cart with its groceries and just walk out.

Things changed for me in 2012. I made a little attempt at killing myself. It wasn't so much that I wanted to kill myself as it was that I was obsessed with the idea of dying. What is it like to die? It was really a weird thing going on in my head. I had a buddy kill himself when I was 17, and he was 18. That made me obsessed with death. For years I thought about killing myself.

One night in 2012 I took a whole bunch of these Celexa. Then after I swallowed them, I realized that I didn't want to die. I called Patty. I talked to her for a while on the phone, and finally I told her what I did.

She said, "Well, don't you think you should call the doctors? Don't you think maybe you should go to the emergency room?"

Then it started striking me that I was going to die. This was real. I was really facing life and death. I chose life. I called 911. They took me down to the hospital where they told me that those pills would not have killed me anyway. They would make me a little sick, but they wouldn't kill me. But while I was in the hospital, the doctors took a hard look at me.

They said I had bipolar disorder. They prescribed two new meds—Lamotrigine (a mood stabilizer) and Abilify (an anti-psychotic which counters depression). So now I was taking four pills every day. I still went up and down, but not as much as before. It helped me to realize that everybody's got their ups and downs.

I had to accept the fact that there is a chemical imbalance in my brain. I had to accept the fact that I had to take these four pills every day. If I wanted to have any chance of staying sober, I had to deal with my mental illness.

This brings to mind DRA—Dual Recovery Anonymous. DRA involves dealing with your mental illness as well as your addiction. If you treat only the alcoholism, then your mental illness fires up. If you treat only the mental illness, then you start drinking again to self-medicate. I realized that I had to to work on both of these at the same time. It was a wonderful program. It helped a lot of people. It was a step beyond AA.

It's been one of the harder things in my life—to accept that I have mental illness. My alcoholism was easy to accept. With 12 DWI's, it was easy to accept. But being mentally ill has a stigma to it. As an alcoholic, I knew I had a stigma. Being a convicted felon is another stigma. Being mentally ill is one more stigma, You feel so defeated. But then you realize that there's a way that I can deal with this. I must achieve and maintain stability.

If I can remain stable, I can start working on the other parts of my life. Until I achieve stability, I can't work on my alcoholism. I can't work on my relationships. Because if my mental illness flares up, what do I do? I drink. That was my answer to everything. When I'm not feeling right, I drink.

When some people hear you have mental illness, they think of you as some sort of freak—like you are going to grow a third head or something. Once I accepted my mental illness, I recognized that I needed to take all four of these medications each day.

### Therapists

I think we should talk about my therapists. I've had two of them since I sobered up - David and then Greta. David understood my problem of alcoholism better than most therapists do. I could say anything to him. I didn't have to worry about being judged. There were some things that I really didn't want to talk about with Steve, my AA sponsor. These I talked over with David.

Then I quit going. For the next year and a half, I didn't have a therapist. Then Beacon got ahold of me and my brother died. I recognized that I really needed a therapist. It was after my brother's death that I got a new therapist—Greta. Greta is just a wonderful young lady. She got me through some major, major problems, like my brother dying. She would sit and listen to me. I would talk about the same thing over and over again. She just let me talk. Once in a while she would poke me a little bit, "What are you feeling?"

Sometimes when she got too close to the bone, I changed the subject. She said I used diversion a lot. I would start talking about something. Then if it became too serious, I would divert. I would change the subject. But Greta saw exactly what I was doing. She is just wonderful. I see how much she has meant to me for the past year and a half, two years now. With Greta I have doctor/patient confidentiality. The only reason that Greta is required to reveal something is because she is a mandated reporter. When you get a job like hers and there is abuse, violence or danger to oneself or others, she needs to report that. But other than that, I can talk to her about anything with complete confidentiality.

I have become an open book. When I first started seeing Greta, I was still pretty closed. But she helped me realize that I am not that different from anyone else. Everybody has depression. Everybody has anxiety. Everybody has good days. Everybody has bad days. It is just a matter of the extreme. She helped me to deal with it – for example, with breathing techniques. So, now if I go into a store and start getting a little panicky, I will stop. I will take a deep breath. I just relax myself. I take these deep breaths and let them out slow. It is amazing. It refocuses me. It is like rebooting yourself. I go in to Greta, and I talk to her about Dawn, about Sue. I talk to Greta about everybody. Greta knows that I have had a life of extremes. She just got her license a few months ago. I figure if she can deal with me, she can deal with anybody. I look forward to my Tuesdays because I know that I am going to go talk to Greta.

Greta is so positive. In the last year and a half, I have done a lot of talking, and we have covered a lot of things. I also see my psychiatrist once in a while for "med checking."

### Learning the basics

There are a number of basic skills that most people take for granted, but I had to learn each of them after I became sober. Let's start with a phone. After I had been sober about six months I got a cheap cell phone. It was a Walmart Straight Talk. I did that for about a year and a half. I figured out how to make voice phone calls and basic text messages.

Then I got together with Dawn. She had this big fancy iPhone. I was kind of jealous, and she said, "Why don't you get on my plan with me?" That's when I got myself a smart phone. That was the first monthly bill that I was responsible for. I was responsible to pay it. This was a bill that came in the mail. "Now I've got a bill that I gotta pay!" That was something new for me.

I was becoming part of society. I had bills. I didn't have a bank account. I just gave Dawn the money. I still don't have a checking account or a savings account. I am sending my money to my sister, Bev, and she is teaching me how to budget. Right now I am not responsible enough to take care of my cash by myself. Bev is teaching me how to budget money. I am 57 years old, and I still don't know how to budget money. I don't know how to do a checkbook. There are so many little things that I don't know.

I had to remember to lock my door. Most people do that automatically. But it took me a while to get used to the idea that I have to lock my door. For years I didn't have a door to lock. I learned to shop for groceries. I don't have any credit cards. I use cash for everything in my life. My sister sends me MasterCard gift cards. They work like a credit card. You give them the card, and it is worth $50.

I knew how to make drunk friends. That was easy. You just start talking to another drunk. But actually learning how to make a friend when I was sober, I had no skills for that. I started by making friends in AA. Sometimes two or three of us would go out after the meeting and have coffee together. To make real male friends required me to pick up that telephone, give somebody a call and say, "Hey, do you want to go out and have a cup of coffee?" That was new to me, and at first it was really hard to do. So, I started forcing myself to invite guys out for coffee. It was hard to learn, but I knew that I had to have male friends. For me finding male friends was harder than finding female friends. With women, I'm kind of a charmer.

### Buses

When I first sobered up, I had spent the last five years in St. Paul, but I didn't know anything about the town. I knew how to get to a couple places on the bus, and that was it. All of a sudden, here I was. I was sober. I needed to get places. So, I started getting bus schedules.

First, I wanted to get to ADAP (the Alcohol and Drug Addiction Program at Regions Hospital). I took the #63 bus. There was a meeting there every Wednesday night. I wanted to get there. I caught the #63 downtown. If I was at Patty's place I would take the #71 bus to downtown and then transfer to the #63. All of the buses originate in downtown.

So, when I moved downtown to the American House, it was so much easier to get around. But it was scary trying to figure out the bus system. I was trying to figure out how to use my phone to tell me where to go. I would get an address, and I would be terrified. I wouldn't go places because I didn't know how to ride the bus. But I started riding the bus more and more. I would go out to Patty's. I would go to ADAP. I would go out to the mall in Maplewood. I began to explore. I would take the #63 out to Grand Avenue and get to know that area a little bit. I took the #70 out to Maple Grove Heights. I started learning where these buses go. I learned to use my phone. I would tell my phone where I wanted to go, and it would tell me what bus to take and what time to leave.

### Dating

It was hard to learn to date. I had never dated in my life. Even as a kid, I never dated. Well, I guess I had one girlfriend before I joined the navy. I had Janet. She was the only girlfriend I had. She lived in one place, and I lived in another place, and we would get together. But mostly generally with the women in my life, I moved in with them. I would get to know them, and I would move right in. Boom. There was no dating involved.

So, when I got sober, I didn't know how to ask a woman out. I didn't know how to bring up the subject of sex. Here I was sober. A guy gets horny. And you don't know how to approach this. I like to be a gentleman. Then, you ask somebody out, and you get rejected. Then you don't feel like doing it again. Dating was hard.

I finally got on a dating website. It was called "Plenty of Fish" (as in "There are plenty of fish in the ocean.") You go through that website. You start texting back and forth, and then you can decide whether you want to give someone your phone number. So with the phone number you can text and make voice phone calls.

I started talking to women. We would chat back and forth on the telephone. I began to get to know them. Of course, you don't know if they are telling you the truth or not. You have never seen them in person. So, you are just talking. I met a lot of really weird women. I met one that just wanted to talk dirty all the time. I met one that was out in left field talking about her prior lives. OK, this was a little too deep for me. I had to wade through them. I went on a few dates with a few different women.

I had some dates. I got these tickets to the Guthrie, and I would take my dates there. We would go out to dinner. I often began by meeting them at my local coffee shop on Grand Avenue, a few blocks from my apartment. This was my ground. I felt a little more secure on my home ground. I walked over there.

One woman that I met was a big executive in an insurance company. We got along pretty good but we lived in such different worlds. There was no way it would work. I dated one woman who started stalking me. She wouldn't leave me alone. And I met Sue. Sue is just a normal, everyday person. She works at a school. She doesn't drink. She is everyday society, but that is still so far out of my realm that I don't know if we can make that work.

Of course Dawn is in my life. Dawn and I are not girlfriend/ boyfriend, but she doesn't go away. She is a true and steady friend. I tell Dawn to go get herself a boyfriend.

### I host a party

When I first moved into my current apartment in October of 2012, I threw a big party. I made meat balls and chicken. I made all sorts of food, and I probably had 15 people here. I was in my glory. I was in my own home. I was having friends over – a bunch of really good friends. And I was feeding them. What more could I look for in life? It was a real high point for me - having my own home and having all these people in my home.

On a regular basis, whenever anyone comes over, the deal is that I cook and they do dishes. I can cook pretty much anything. I do really well with chicken breasts. I don't eat much red meat. I eat pork chops, chicken, and fish. I know people are always happy to come over.

### Connecting with my children

I had been sober for a couple of years, and I was on Facebook a lot. My son Jeremy had sobered up. He had been sober for about a year, and he was watching me on Facebook. He finally contacted me, and we started talking. Here we were–two sober men. We talked more and more. Josh joined the conversation. We talked on the telephone. Now I was talking with each of them on the phone. We were all on edge, not knowing what we were getting into. Sometimes when I talked with Jeremy or Josh, it was touchy. We didn't know what to say to each other. When they invited me

**This 2015 photo shows my son Jeremy and his family. Left to right: Hailey (16), Jeremy's wife Ellie holding Will (2 ½), my son Jeremy, and Bailey (16). In the front are Johanna (9) and Jacob (7).**

out to visit them in Portland Oregon, I was all excited. I was going to meet my grandkids. I had saved up enough money to buy a plane ticket. I got on that airplane. I had a round trip ticket for a ten-day visit. It was 2013. I got on that plane and I started thinking. I've got two sons in Oregon that I don't know. They are not kids anymore. They are men. They were 31 and 30 years old. I started getting worried. How is this going to go? Do they really want me to be there? Or are they just being nice?

I got off that airplane, and I started walking toward baggage claim. There was Jeremy with his wife Ellie and little Will, my youngest grandson. And I knew everything was going to be alright. Jeremy gave me a big hug. I just knew it was going to be OK.

I talked with the boys until the wee hours of the morning. We talked about different things—about their mom, about me, what's happened with them, what's happened with me. There was so much ground to cover. We found out that we still loved each other. And they both called me "Dad." To my ears that was the sweetest music ever. That and hearing little Will shout, "Papa." It just melted me.

Both my boys were doing really well for themselves. They both had good jobs. They were not drinking, not using. They were both pretty messed up as kids. Jeremy was into the meth and drinking. Josh was drinking and smoking dope. I learned that my wife had kicked Jeremy out of the house when he was 14 years old. He lived on the streets, stayed with friends. He followed in my footsteps a lot. But he sobered up after he turned 30. Josh took care of his mom. She used to drink and smoke weed with them when they were 13 years old. She had severe mental illness. She would threaten to kill herself every time Josh said he was going to move out. She manipulated him into staying with her for a long time, and finally he went to Hawaii to get away from her. But he still had to send her money so she could buy her medications.

### REGULAR VISITS WITH MY FAMILY

I am very, very proud of both of my boys and grandkids. The love I have for them—well, I am not real sure what love is, but I know what I feel for my kids and my grandkids. On my last visit I took out my 15-year-old granddaughter. We went out together one night and had sushi and hung out. It was comfortable. I didn't know what I was going to talk about with this 15-year-old, but we just talked. She opened up with me. It was just a special, special night. This was the beautiful little baby in a red dress whose picture I first saw in prison. I didn't meet her in person until she was a teenager.

Being around my children is the high point of my life. It is something that I have wanted since they disappeared back in 1991. I wanted to be in my kids' lives—to have them back in my life and hear "I love you, Dad" every time we talk on the phone. It's wonderful to know that I am accepted and welcomed out there. I love to hold my grandkids. To get a family picture of me with my five grandbabies it is one of the sweetest things I've ever done. I can't say enough about the love that I have gotten back from these kids. I really don't deserve it, but they give it to me. They respect me as a human being. Sometimes things are touchy. We have our differences, and I don't know them that well yet. I am just getting to know them. But I wouldn't trade this for anything on earth. I love my kids. I love my grandkids. That is one of the big reasons that I stay sober. Because I don't want to lose them again.

It has been a year since I have been out there. Will was 1½ then. He is 2½ now. Last year Will was just beginning to talk. I would start putting on my shoes, getting ready to go outside and have a cigarette. Little Will would get excited, and he would come running to me. He would know that I was about to go outside. He would say, "Papa! Outside? Papa! Outside?" He would grab my finger with his hand and pull me around.

### I have recreated myself

It is so important for me to do things that are the "new me." I have recreated myself. It is not a chance that many people get in life —to recreate themselves. When I moved into American House, I learned that there were free tickets to the Guthrie Theater. I knew very little about the Guthrie. I knew it was a playhouse. I didn't realize what a good playhouse it was. I got four tickets. I got all fancy dressed up, and I took three friends. When I got there, it was pretty casual. Some people dress up fancy, but some people came in blue jeans.

The first time I was pretty uptight about what is it going to be like—being around these rich people? Only rich people go to the Guthrie! Just the fancy people! I found out that every time I went to the Guthrie, I got more comfortable.

Now I know my way around the Guthrie. I bring new people all the time with these free tickets I get. I show them around the

Guthrie. I take them up to the Yellow Room. I show them the Endless Bridge. I know the place. And it is really fun to be able to do this with people. I call them "Guthrie Virgins." I have taken at least 20 friends to the Guthrie and most of them were Guthrie Virgins. Just about every time I go, I take somebody who hasn't been there. Sometimes I see the same play as many as four times.

I have a friend in town, Tosha. I think of her as my daughter. She is actually the daughter of my friend, Patty. Tosha is into the arts. She is always real happy to go. I get four tickets, and I try to take a different woman, and she takes a different guy—just to show them the theater—what live theater is all about. I thought that when I went to the Guthrie everybody would look at me like they knew that I used to be a bum—a drunken bum. But they didn't look at me. I was accepted like everybody else. I am loving live theater.

Last week I saw "Disgraced." It's about a guy from Pakistan. He is second generation, and he tells everyone he is from India because during his father's day it was India. But his employer found out that he was from Pakistan. His employer started questioning whether he was from Pakistan and whether he was a Muslim. He was Muslim but he was against his religion. In fact, he was fighting with his nephew who was kind of into the Jihad, and the nephew was thinking about going back to where he came from. This guy ends up getting fired from his job, losing his wife and it is all over his religion. It is a very good play.

Recently I have also been to the symphony. Somebody took me. I loved it. Somebody took me there to show me another side of culture. I don't own a suit, but I dress up in a pair of khakis and a nice black shirt. That's dressed up for me.

Several months ago I got summoned to jury duty. Most people take jury duty as a burden. ...."Aaahhh, I gotta do jury duty." But when I got that summons to go to jury duty, I laughed. Six years ago I was living on the streets, a drunken felon. Now they want me to come and serve on jury duty. It was so ironic.

I called the office and told them that I was a felon. They asked, "Are you on parole?"

I said, "No."

They said, "Well, then, we don't care. You are being summoned for jury duty." I was excited about serving on jury duty. I appeared at the courtroom each day waiting to be called. Being summoned to jury duty was just one more step back into society. It's like I took a big leap there from being homeless to being established as a citizen of this country now. It was a special treat. I was never called for a jury, so I didn't get to serve. But still, to me, it was a really big thing. It was a privilege. It made me feel good.

I was very honored to be a featured speaker at the Minneapolis Convention Center before one thousand people. I believe in what Beacon Interfaith Housing Collaborative does. They are trying to end homelessness in the Twin Cities. They asked me to speak for them. I agreed. I didn't know there were going to be a thousand people there. They told me that afterwards. But they coached me and rehearsed me. We timed everything out. It is a very scheduled thing. I had 3½ minutes. So, we got my speech down to 3½ minutes. We practiced and practiced. I would read it into the mirror. I wanted to do this right. I was getting in front of a bunch of people trying to tell them that we need to help the homeless. I got up there, and I was very comfortable. It just came natural to me.

When the luncheon ended a number of people came up to talk to me. The Beacon people asked me to speak at their luncheon the second year. It was more of an update of what was going on in my life. I let people know that things just kept getting better. I believe there is no end to "better." People would come and talk to me afterwards. It was rewarding for me to know that I am doing my tiny, small part—trying to do something about homelessness.

### GIVING BACK

Alice is my older cousin. She is in her early 70's, she lives here in St. Paul with her great granddaughter that she is raising. She has no money. She told me that her sink was dripping, dripping. So I told her I would come over and look at it. I fixed it. All it needed was new baskets. Alice was ever so grateful. She tried to pay me a bunch of money but I turned her down and told her I didn't need it. I actually needed the money, but I didn't want to take her money. She probably needed it more than I.

I like to think that taking people into my home is an important way for me to give back. I have taken at least a half dozen people into my home in this apartment in the last three or four years. Each of them has a unique story, but what they all have in common is that I met them through AA and each was desperate for a temporary place to stay. I have a one bedroom, one bath apartment, but I invited them to come home with me and sleep on my couch.

Chuck is a good example. I met Chuck through AA, and I learned that he had lost everything. He was homeless and he didn't even have a place for his cat. So, I invited Chuck to stay with me. He brought his cat "Rabbit." They both stayed here for about four months. As long as he was sitting here in my house, he wasn't doing anything constructive. I finally said, "You've got to go, Chuck. You have to find yourself a place to live and get on with your life." I felt that I had helped him as much as I could. It was time for him to move on. He did.

Chuck found a place where he had outpatient treatment, and he has stayed sober ever since. He went from my place to a halfway house to a sober house to his own apartment in only 14 months. Now he has a part time job, and he's sober. I still have his cat. The cat named Rabbit has turned into my little sweetheart. I never wanted a cat. I still don't want a cat, but I want Rabbit. I am going to be sorry to give up Rabbit. I am attached to her. I feel like I was part of Chuck's recovery.

Then there was Jamie from Anchorage, Alaska. She was a very attractive, petite blonde woman. She came to Minnesota for treatment. Minnesota is known as a "mecca of recovery." It's a magnet for people who need to get sober. I met Jamie in AA. She was young. She could have been my daughter. She was having troubles, married to this guy, in and out of recovery. Finally, she realized that she had lost everything. She didn't have a place to lay her head down – without sleeping with some guy. She was talking to me, and I said, "Jamie, come and sleep on my couch. You need to figure out your life." I told her she could stay with me, but there was one rule. "No drinking. Simple as that. If you drink, you gotta go."

That night she phoned me from a bar. She said, "John, can I really do this?"

I said, "Yeah, Jamie. I will buy you your last beer, and you can come and stay with me." So I went into the bar, bought her a beer, and she walked with me over to my apartment. She stayed with me for a couple of weeks. Then she got herself into a halfway house. Then she went back to Alaska. She is doing really well up there. She has a new baby

There was a gal from Chicago. There was a guy from North Carolina. These are all people I met in AA. They had lost everything and had no place to go. I let them come and stay with me and get started again. I give them a week to try to figure out what they are going to do. I feel that this is really giving back. It gives them a little hope when they are invited some place. Not only do they have a roof over their head, but they know that someone actually cares about them. That is just as important.

Taking care of my dying brother was the toughest thing I've ever done. I found out that my brother Bruce was dying of cancer about three years before he passed. But he was doing well at the time. They got the colon cancer, but he never said a lot about his lung cancer. He fought with it. Finally he told me that he had only a few months left. I dropped everything. I had seen him the week before I spoke at the Beacon luncheon. At that time I told him, "Bruce, if you need me, I'll come."

He was living in Park Rapids, and he said, "I could have used you a week ago." I knew that meant he really needed me. But I had this commitment to speak for Beacon, and I had to go through with that. After the Beacon luncheon I went up north immediately. I moved Bruce from Park Rapids to Oaklee. Until then I had not realized how bad Bruce was. Now I knew he didn't have a couple of months. He was coughing out a bunch of blood. Three days after moving him to Oaklee, he was dead. It was the most horrible thing to watch – somebody dying of lung cancer. Bruce and I were so close. When I was with him those last days, he couldn't talk. But I was there. I talked to him. I held his hand. I fed him his morphine. Here I was - a dope addict with these bottles of morphine, and I never once considered taking any myself. It was the worst experience of my life, but I will never regret it because I was there for my brother.

### MY BUCKET LIST

The first thing on my bucket list is finishing this book. I hope it is a positive story painting a picture of hope for recovery. I suppose if I can stop drinking and start recreating myself, anyone can do it. I hope my story will give a voice to the homeless. I especially hope that it will be helpful to kind and generous people who want to deal with homelessness.

This book has been a big focus of my life for the past year, but when the book is finished, I will need a new focus. Here are some other things on my bucket list.

First of all, I would like to talk with my wife—not to scream and holler at her. I don't want to do that. But I want to tell her how I feel—about how I was never a good husband to her. I would like for her and me to sit down with the kids and have a holiday together. Up until now Betty has refused to talk to me. She can't get over her anger. I would like to make some amends to her. It would be so wonderful for Betty and me to sit down with our grandkids.

We never got a divorce, I have been legally married to her since 1991. I would like to get an official divorce so that we can both move on with our lives. After I became sober, I wrote a letter to her. I didn't know where to send it, so it was never sent, but it helped me a lot. It helped me figure out how I was really feeling. Perhaps I could give a letter to my son, and he could give it to her without me ever knowing her address. Betty is a touchy subject for me. I still care for her. She is the mother of my children. I care what happens to her. I truly wish she could find the happiness that I have found.

Second, I am looking forward to riding the Empire Builder Amtrak train to the West Coast. I have wanted to ride on the Amtrak all my life. I have taken that journey countless times on freight trains, and I used to joke about why pay for something you can get for free. But I must admit that for years I looked at those people whizzing by on Amtrak trains—relaxing, eating nice meals, putting their seats back. Deep down I envied them. Now I want to be one of those people.

Third, I want to go to Alaska. My thought is to take the Amtrak to Seattle and take a ferry boat up to Alaska, just for the adventure. I need adventure in my life.

Fourth, there is my trip to Maine when I didn't get to eat lobster. I still want to go to Bar Harbor, Maine and eat a lobster. I don't especially like lobster, but it is just the idea—Maine and lobster.

Fifth, I sometimes feel like I should be doing more—get a full time job. But for a 57-year-old felon it's not easy to find a job. People look at my record, and they shake their head at me.

But I am going to keep plugging. I am going to find something that I am comfortable with. I planted a seed with Beacon that I would like to go to work for them. I would really like to work with the homeless.

Made in the USA
Middletown, DE
25 January 2017